BEYOND THE WAND

BEYOND THE WAND

THE MAGIC AND MAYHEM OF GROWING UP A WIZARD

TOM FELTON

EBURY SPOTLIGHT

10

Ebury Spotlight, an imprint of Ebury Publishing
20 Vauxhall Bridge Road
London SW1V 2SA

Ebury Spotlight is part of the Penguin Random House group of companies
whose addresses can be found at global.penguinrandomhouse.com

All images from the author's private collection or reproduced
with kind permission of the following rights holders:

Abacus Agency. Warner Bros (Licensed By: Warner Bros. Entertainment Inc. All rights reserved.). Total Carp magazine. Getty Images (Dave Benett / Contributor). PA Images (Alamy Stock Photo). Amy Stares. Getty Images (Kevin Winter / Staff). Getty Images (Stephen Lovekin / Staff). Twentieth Century Fox ('RISE OF THE PLANET OF THE APES' © 2011 Twentieth Century Fox. All rights reserved). Alamy (© 20TH CENTURY FOX / Album). Alamy (Collection Christophel © 2011 Tandem Productions GmbH & F / DR Photo Kelly Walsh). Sony (RISEN © 2016. Fifty Days Productions LLC. All Rights Reserved. Courtesy of Columbia Pictures. Alamy (Rosie Collins / © Sony Pictures Releasing / courtesy Everett Collection). Twentieth Century Fox and Pathe ('A UNITED KINGDOM' ©2016 Pathe Productions Limited, British Broadcasting Corporation and British Film Institute. All rights reserved. Still provided courtesy of Twentieth Century Fox and Pathe). Alamy (Prod DB © Film United - Harbinger Pictures - Pathe / DR A UNITED KINGDOM de Amma Asante 2016 GB/USA/TCH). © IFC Films / Covert Media. Alamy (Dusan Martinicek / © IFC Films / courtesy Everett Collection). Alamy (Levitate Film / Caviar Films / Album). Nick Rutter.

First published by Ebury Spotlight in 2022

www.penguin.co.uk

A CIP catalogue record for this book is available from the British Library

ISBN 9781529149418
ISBN TPB 9781529149425

Printed and bound in Great Britain by Clays Ltd, Elcograf S.p.A.
Imported into the EEA by Penguin Random House Ireland,
Morrison Chambers, 32 Nassau Street, Dublin D02 YH68

Penguin Random House is committed to a sustainable future for our business, our readers and
our planet. This book is made from Forest Stewardship Council® certified paper.

I dedicate this book to the Muggles who got me here.

Contents

Foreword

by Emma Watson

You know that person in your life who makes you feel seen? That person who is somehow a witness to all that unfolds? That person who knows – really *knows* – what is happening to you and what you're going through, without anything having to be said?

For me, that person is Tom Felton.

As you'll read in this book, our relationship didn't start well. When we first met, I was a moony and probably rather annoying nine-year-old girl who followed him round like a puppy, desperate for his attention. But, as he has written so eloquently, beautifully and generously in this book, our friendship didn't end there. Thank goodness it blossomed and endured.

If you could boil the Harry Potter stories down to a single idea (and there are so many I am really stretching here), it would surely be about the value of friendship and how nothing of true meaning can be achieved without it. Friendships are the lynchpin of human existence, and I am so thankful that at crucial turning points in my life, Tom has been there to reassure and understand me. The friendship we share has allowed me to move through some of the most challenging and soul-searching moments in my life.

But enough about me. This book is about Tom. He has a heart the size of a planet. I've never really witnessed anything like it, except perhaps in his mum, Sharon. The Felton factor is real. You'll read a lot in this book about Tom's brother Chris, who was a regular face on the Harry Potter set, and who is one of the funniest people I've ever met. The whole family is special and Tom, the youngest of four brothers, has inherited their kindness and down-to-earth nature.

Which means that if you meet Tom, you meet the *real* Tom. That's not the case with all actors. The vast majority put on a persona when they meet the public. It's like flicking a switch: they're very professional, they do it extremely well and the person they're greeting will never know the difference. But it's not the real them. It's a routine. Tom doesn't do that. Tom is always Tom. He doesn't flick a switch. There *is* no switch. What you see is what you get. He is incredibly generous with his fans and with the wider Harry Potter community. That special ability he has to make *me* feel seen extends to everybody. He might have played a bully. He might even have sometimes felt like a bully. But take it from me: he couldn't be further from one. He is creative, sensitive and whole-hearted. He is a person who wants to love everything and everyone.

Socrates said that the unexamined life is not worth living. When I look at how honestly Tom has reflected on his life and experiences in this book, I'm reminded that he has an astonishing amount of self-awareness. He has been able to laugh at himself as well as relive moments in his life that have been difficult and painful for him. He is on a journey of self-work, and I'm with Socrates when I say that the people who are on that journey are the only people for me. But Tom has gone one step further than most: he has unpacked that journey for us, his readers. It is such a generous act, especially in this world of social media and instant news, where the polarity of opinions makes it such an intense time to lay yourself bare in the way that he has. You want to live a real, a truthful, an examined life, and Tom clearly does.

Like Tom, I always struggle to explain to people the nature of our connection and relationship. For more than twenty years now we've loved each other in a special way, and I've lost count of the times that people have said to me, 'You must have drunkenly made out, just once!' 'You must have kissed!' 'There must be something!' But what we have is far deeper than that. It's one of the purest loves I can think of. We're soulmates, and we've always had each other's backs. I know we always will. It makes me emotional to think about it. Sometimes it feels hard to live in a world where people are so quick to judge, to doubt, to question intentions. Tom doesn't do that. I know that, even if I've made a mistake, he'll understand that my intention was good. I know that he'll always *believe* me. Even when he doesn't have the whole picture, he'll never doubt that I'm coming from a good place and will have done my very best. That's *true* friendship, and to be seen and loved like that is one of the great gifts of my life.

We have always shared a love of words, of how they can be used better to express oneself. Tom, you're a poet. The way your mind works and the way you express things is beautiful, charming, funny and warm. I'm so glad that you have written this book and shared it with us. It's a delight and a gift. The world is lucky to have you, but I'm even luckier to have you as my friend.

Chapeau, little piece of my soul. And congratulations.

Emma Watson
London, 2022

1

UNDESIRABLE NO. 1

or

DRACO'S FIRST SCRAPE WITH THE LAW

Cards on the table: this is not going to be my proudest moment. In fact, my mum doesn't even know this story. So, sorry Mum.

It's a busy Saturday afternoon in a bustling English town. Punters hurriedly go about their business and clusters of teenagers haunt the shopping centres, doing what teenagers do. They pay no attention to a skinny fourteen-year-old boy with a pale complexion and bleached hair loitering in the vicinity, surrounded by his crew. The boy in question is yours truly and I'm genuinely sorry to report that we had trouble in mind.

You might think - and rightly so - that with my distinctive blond hairdo I'd be well advised to *avoid* trouble. You might think that trouble would be low on my agenda. But it turns out that regular teenagers don't always do the right thing - they certainly don't always do the *sensible* thing - and I am trying very hard to be just that: a regular teenager.

Which is not always entirely straightforward, when your alter ego is a wizard.

• • •

This was early on in my wizarding career, between the first and second Potter films. The object of our attention was the HMV record store in Guildford, Surrey - quite the place to hang out back in the day. It was commonplace for kids to swipe CDs from their cases and walk out with them under their coats, a constant challenge for the poor security guards who paced the aisles looking for scallywags up to no good. On this particular Saturday, though, my crew had a bigger prize in its sights than mere CDs: a DVD of an 'adult' nature that none of us were remotely old enough to buy. I wince now to remember it. Truth to tell, I was inwardly wincing then, but I didn't want to show it because I was trying to fit in with the cool kids. Even the top boys were reluctant to commit a crime of this gravity, with all the potential for extreme embarrassment.

Which was why I volunteered to do the deed.

Reader, the Artful Dodger I was not. Palms sweating, pulse racing, I entered the shop with excruciating casualness. The smart move would have been to identify the prize, swipe it and get out of there as quickly as possible. Maybe if I had a bit more Slytherin cunning about me I'd have done just that. But I didn't. Rather than execute a swift, subtle theft, I located the DVD and then I stalked it. I must have wandered up and down the aisle fifty times, my skin tingling with apprehension. I even asked a random stranger if they would buy the DVD for me so I could feign success with the cool kids. The stranger rightly refused and I continued my stakeout, up and down the aisle.

Up and down ...

Up and down ...

An hour must have passed. I honestly doubt that there was a single security guard who hadn't clocked me by now. Whether they'd recognised the world's most inept shoplifter as the boy from the Harry Potter films, I couldn't tell you. What I do know is this: my hairdo was distinctive, if not downright weird. It was a beacon, and it made it impossible for me to melt into the background.

I wished I hadn't volunteered. I knew it was stupid. But I couldn't face tucking my tail between my legs and leaving the shop empty-handed, so eventually I took a deep breath and went in for the dive. Pretending to look at the ceiling, with sweaty, fumbling fingers clumsily ripping off the security sticker, I removed the shiny disc from its plastic box, slipped it into a pocket and speed-walked to the exit.

I'd done the deed! I could see my crew outside and gave them a knowing smirk. I could sense their excitement.

Then ... disaster!

I'd barely taken a single step outside the shop when three burly security guys surrounded me. My stomach turned to ice as they escorted me - politely but ever so firmly - back inside. I made the walk of shame through the store, head down, all eyes on me, desperately hoping that I wouldn't be recognised. The characters were not so iconic then, but there was always a chance. The guards led me into a little booth at the back of the store, where they stood around me, grim-faced, and asked me to turn out my pockets. I sheepishly handed over the disc and asked them - *begged* them - not to do the one thing that would make this whole sorry escapade ten times worse. 'Please,' I said, '*please* don't tell my mum!' If she found out, the humiliation would be unbearable.

They didn't tell my mum. But they did put me against the wall, bring out a Polaroid camera and take an instant snapshot of my face. They put the Polaroid on the wall, part of a rogue's gallery of hardened criminals who'd tried to rip off the record store, and they told me I was barred for life. I could never set foot in HMV again.

No chance of that, mate. Cheeks burning, I hoofed it as fast as I could and didn't look back. My friends had scarpered at the first sight of security, so I took the train home alone to lie low.

• • •

How long did that picture of blond Tom hang on the wall of HMV? Who knows? Maybe it's still there. But for weeks after that I was terrified that Warner Brothers, or the newspapers, would find out about my stupid indiscretion. I never told a single soul, but what would happen if someone recognised my mugshot? Would they fire me? Would the next film see Harry, Ron and Hermione terrorised by a different Draco? Would the humiliating nature of my brush with the law become hilarious fodder for public consumption?

Like I said, I tried very hard to be a regular teenager. In most respects, even despite everything that the future held, I think I managed it pretty well. But there's a fine line, when you grow up in the public eye, between being normal and being reckless. I crossed the line that Saturday afternoon, no doubt. And while the young Tom Felton was no Draco Malfoy, he was no saint either. Maybe that's what got me the part in the first place. I'll let you be the judge of that.

• • •

Oh, and we never did get to watch that DVD.

2

MY MUGGLE FAMILY

or

RUNT OF THE PACK

Draco Malfoy, the character for whom I would become most famous for portraying, was an only child, born to a cold and brutal family. My own family couldn't have been more different. Close-knit, loving, chaotic and supportive, they were the very centre of my early life. I'm the youngest of four brothers, and before I introduce you to my mum and dad, I want to tell you about my three siblings. They each influenced me profoundly in different ways, and I would have been a very different character without them.

My bros will gladly tell you that I'm the runt of the pack. At least, that's what they kindly used to tell me. (I *think* they were joking, but you know how it is with brothers.) I'm the youngest of the four. Jonathan, Christopher and Ashley came along in a cluster, three boys in the space of four years. Then there were six years of respite for my mum before I arrived on 22 September 1987. So from the moment I entered the world I had three older brothers to keep my butt off the couch and my fingers away from the TV remote. Three older brothers to bully me with love. Three older brothers to joke that I came along so late not because I was an afterthought but because I was in fact the milkman's son. (They were, and still are, considerably bigger than me, all six-foot-plus and built like brick shithouses.) In short, three older guys to keep me firmly in my place - which I guess is no bad thing for a kid who's about to embark on a wizarding career.

My brothers didn't only call me 'runt'. If they were feeling generous they might also refer to me as 'maggot'. But it wasn't all bad; they also each had a massive positive influence on me throughout my unusual childhood, although in slightly different ways.

Jonathan - we call him Jink - is the eldest and, back in the day, it was he who first showed me by example that it was cool to have a passion for the arts. Jink was the one with the Oasis poster on his wall and the black Stratocaster - or at least a knock-off version of a Strat - in his bedroom. He was into music, singing and performing - pursuits that plenty of kids don't always get encouraged to do. That might have happened to me had it not been for Jink. When I was very young, he went to acting classes and I would go with my family to see him on stage. The actors were only kids, none of them older than their early teens, and let's be frank: these were not slick, professional shows. Jink is a chiropractor now - a talent wasted, as he reminds me frequently - but he is also a deeply creative guy. I remember watching him in musicals like *South Pacific, West Side Story, Guys and Dolls* and, most memorably, *Little Shop of Horrors*. It was while sitting in those audiences, wide-eyed, that I learned an important and formative lesson: it wasn't weird to do this stuff and it looked like fun. Seeing my big brother up there taught me that it's okay to want to perform, no matter what other people think.

So, nice one, Jink. Which brings us to brother number two.

Chris? Total opposite. 'Acting's lame, bruv! Dancing? Fuck off!'

Chris is the second oldest of the Felton foursome and would no more put on a pink leotard and pretend to be the Fairy Godmother than he would fly. Which I have to tell you is a shame, because he would look tip-top in a tutu. Whereas Jink is slightly more sensitive to the emotional shifts of those around him, with Chris, what you see is what you get. So perhaps it's unexpected that Chris should be the brother I was closest to during the Potter years, the brother who looked after me, kept me grounded and was the biggest influence on the teenage Tom. Chris chaperoned me for two-and-a-half Potter films. I say chaperoned, but what I really mean is that he slept in the trailer and made full use of the free on-set catering - more of which later. For now, suffice to say that Chris didn't always take his chaperoning duties entirely seriously. On a fairly regular basis, we used to leave set at 8pm and drive over an hour from the studios, straight down to our local fishery. We'd set up our tent, cast our rods and enjoy a night's fishing. Then, at six in the morning we'd reel in, pack up our gear, head back (slightly muddy) to set and pretend to the nice people at Warner Brothers that I'd been at home sleeping soundly all night. So if you think that Draco occasionally looked a little pale, it wasn't just down to the make-up department.

There was a time at which in my eyes - in most people's eyes, I suppose - there seemed no doubt that Chris would become the most famous Felton. His claim to fame? He was one of England's most up-and-coming carp anglers. There is a tight-knit community of these carp anglers, and among them Chris was very much one to watch. He made the cover of *Carp Talk* and *Big Carp* magazines several times for catching famous fish in famous lakes, which worked in my favour among my contemporaries who were into angling. They massively looked up to him and I was definitely considered cooler because of my association with him. And since I looked up to him too, we used to go fishing together pretty much any time that we had off. It must have been tough for him when Potter changed all our lives: one minute he's known for being one of Britain's best fishermen, the next minute everyone's calling him Draco Malfoy's brother and shouting 'On yer broom-stick, mate!' Chris took it in his stride, though, and despite everything that came my way he was truly my hero as I was growing up. He introduced me to lots of music - Bob Marley, the Prodigy, Marvin Gaye and 2Pac - which would become one of my lifelong passions. He introduced me to other less innocent pastimes, too. We'll get to that. Fishing, though, was our obsession.

Thanks to Chris I was a regular fixture at Bury Hill Fisheries in Surrey, and I even had a weekend job there in the very early days of Potter, which I took for a little extra pocket money and the promise of free fishing. My main gig was to help with the parking, so every Saturday and Sunday I'd be there at six in the morning guiding eager fishermen into the tiny car park, hiding my bleached-blond Malfoy hair under a fishing beanie. Afterwards, I'd snag myself a bacon sandwich before doing the rounds of the lake with a brown leather satchel full of coins, selling tickets to the anglers.

I was not, I should say, the most conscientious worker. On one occasion I went back to Chris's flat to watch a big boxing match that was being shown in the UK at four in the morning. I was so excited, and managed to stay up right to the moment that the boxing match started, at which point little tiny twelve-year-old Tom conked out. My brother woke me two hours later to go to work. I made it in, but I got woken up for a second time when the owner found me snoozing under a tree. Meantime, the clients had helped themselves to the car park and the whole place was a complete mess. Sorry, boss.

You might think the punters at the fishery would have found it odd to have Draco Malfoy telling them where to put their 4x4s and collecting their money, but I managed to remain fairly anonymous. In fact, I can count on one hand the number of times I was recognised. The clientele at the fishery was a very particular type of grumpy old man, or so it seemed to me at the time. None of them would have recognised me and, let me tell you, the number of teenage girls rocking up to catch carp at dawn on a Saturday morning was limited. Occasionally a journalist would turn up and write something about my Muggle gig, and from time to time the owner of the fishery wasn't beyond drumming up a little publicity of his own. But on the whole I was left to enjoy the job. And I did enjoy it, not because of the twenty pounds cash-in-hand that I'd receive at the end of each working day, but because of the free fishing. That was the main draw for Chris and me. We were obsessed with the fish, of course, but we were even more obsessed with everything that went with them: the moon and the stars, the proximity of nature, the rods, the reels, the bivvies and, of course, the boilies. Boilies are a type of fish bait the size of a large marble that you cook up in the kitchen with all kinds of disgusting, foul-smelling flavours like squid liver and double monster crab - items that wouldn't be out of place in a Potions lesson. We used to cook up the boilies at home to Mum's complete exasperation at the mess and the stench, swearing blind that we really *would* clear it all up, before heading out to our beloved fishery.

My third brother, closest to me in age and so in some ways the brother with whom I shared most of my early life, is Ash. Unlike my older brothers, we were close enough in age to be at the same school at the same time. (And put it this way: it's useful having an older brother on site, especially if they're built like Ash was then.) Ash and I share a very particular sense of humour; we were forever watching *The Simpsons* or *Beavis and Butt-Head* together. Even now I speak to him more in the voice of Beavis than in my own voice. We sometimes have to rein it back when we're in public. We played sports together - after watching *Space Jam* we pestered my dad to make a basketball hoop in the garden, and after watching *The Mighty Ducks* we had a phase of wanting to be ice hockey players.

Ash has a huge heart, my favourite sense of humour and is one of the nicest guys in the world, but he suffered massively from big swings of emotion in his early teens, to the extent that as he hit adolescence he stopped wanting to go to school or even leave the house. His constant feeling of not being quite happy with who he was meant he ended up spending long periods of time on closed hospital wards. I remember frequently visiting him after school at a hospital in Guildford. I'd like to say that I approached those visits with sensitivity and patience, but I was young and I don't suppose I fully understood what was going on, so really I just remember asking my mum when we could leave.

By the time Ash was feeling better and able to come home, we thankfully got back to having a laugh together. But his teenage difficulties foreshadowed the mental health struggles of the remaining Felton brothers - myself included. More on that later, but for now let's remember that such a predisposition exists among us, and some problems are too difficult to outrun. They always catch up with you in the end.

So there you have it: three older brothers, each of them close to me in their different ways. I'm acutely aware that my involvement with Potter has affected their lives irreversibly: they'll forever, at some level, be known as Draco Malfoy's brothers. But I'm equally aware that each of them exerted a distinct influence over the young Tom. Jink: the creativity and love of performance. Chris: a passion for the outdoors and a down-to-earth nature. Ash: a sense of humour and an early inkling that there is no light without shade. All important life lessons. And while I might well be the maggot - the runt of the pack - I wouldn't be the person I am today without them.

• • •

Like lots of kids, I pinged from one enthusiasm to another. And one of my greatest advantages in life was that I had a mum who encouraged me, but put no undue pressure on me to stick with any one thing.

We had a comfortable upbringing in a pleasant house called Redleaf, opposite a farm in Surrey. It was a happy, buzzy, homely place. We never had loads of money. Our weekly treat was a trip to Dorking car boot sale where twenty pence could get you pretty far and if you had fifty pence in your pocket you were laughing. I'm sure my dad - a hard-working civil engineer - will forgive me for saying that he's famously careful with his money. I've seen him haggle in charity shops! It's the reason I never spent a day hungry, of course, but I think it became a tension between my parents in the later years of their marriage. My mum would be the one saying, 'I really think we need to get Tom a violin, he says he wants to learn.' To which Dad would reply, not unreasonably, 'We only just bought him a hockey stick! Is he done with the hockey now?'

And the answer was, yes, I probably was done with the hockey. I'd moved on, seen something else that caught my eye, like a magpie distracted by a new shiny object. It drove my dad to distraction but my mum was excited by each new passion, however fleeting, and determined not to let my enthusiasm diminish. I never had a moment's hassle or judgement from her when the latest attraction inevitably waned; no raised eyebrow when, three months after taking receipt of my violin, I started skipping violin lessons by hiding in the boys' toilets and instead became obsessed with my cool new yoyo. I wouldn't have blamed my dad for wanting to clobber that violin over the back of my head. Mum, though, was happy encouraging me to be the kind of boy who had passions without forcing me to stick to them once something new came along.

That's not to say Dad didn't take an interest. He absolutely did. He was great at building things and if we wanted something, he'd try to make it. He built us an elaborate basketball hoop, a hockey net and even installed a skateboard ramp in the garden after consulting with us to find out exactly what we wanted. He was often to be found in the shed at midnight, sawing away, making us these amazing things, often out of materials 'borrowed' from the local dump.

There were some items, though, that he couldn't make, and even if he could we didn't want his homemade effort. We wanted the shiny one with the label that all our friends had. It was up to Mum to fund these objects of desire, so, on top of looking after four boys (five, including my dad), she found the time to work multiple jobs to earn the extra cash. She worked for the local estate agent, but she also stacked shelves and cleaned offices at night with her friend Sally - we call her Auntie Sally - who's always been a part of my life and even chaperoned me on set for a while. All this just because I wanted a new yoyo or Ash wanted a basketball with the Air Jordan logo on it rather than the one that sold for a fifth of the price in Woolworths. Whatever it was that caught our eye, Mum did what she could to make it a reality.

Bottom line: my mum is a huge reason I am where I am, even though she never pushed me in the direction of being an actor. I could have set my eyes on being a professional violinist, or ice hockey goalkeeper, or an extreme yoyoist. It wouldn't have mattered to her which activity I ended up pursuing, but one thing's for certain: whatever it was, Mum would have helped me achieve it.

Dad was and is the joker of the pack. He loves not to take himself too seriously and always finds some way to make a joke or slip in some sort of self-deprecating humour. Think Del Boy, Blackadder and Basil Fawlty rolled into one. It's a trait I inherited from him and which I still use to this day. In my line of work, you often find yourself in situations where you meet new people and the ice needs breaking fast. I always try to exercise a little disarming humour, a little buffoonery, which is a technique I learned from my dad.

Dad's job as a civil engineer meant dealing with large building projects at sites all around the world, which in turn meant that he was sometimes away from home. As I grew older, however, his work took him away from home even more. That absence only became more apparent when he and my mum split up. They were married for twenty-five years and I certainly remember them being affectionate, especially during our yearly camping holidays. I remember them calling each other 'honey bear' and 'darling'. It went from that to me sitting on the staircase hearing something quite different - not fights, but exchanges that revealed a definite lack of closeness. Around the time of the first Harry Potter film I remember my mum driving me into school and telling me, quite matter-of-factly: 'Your father and I are getting a divorce.' There was no big song and dance. It was a classically British, pragmatic moment. And I don't recall feeling any great sense of distress at the time, or anger when my mum told me Dad had met someone else. I was only twelve years old, after all, and likely more concerned about which girl I was going to try to chat up in the playground that day.

After that, Dad moved out during the week and returned home at the weekends, when Mum would leave to stay with her sister, my auntie Lindy. An unusual set-up, I guess, which lasted for a couple of years. It was great for us as teenagers because it meant, come the weekend, that we could get away with pretty much anything. When Mum was around, you could barely tap a cigarette box within half a mile without her shouting, 'What are you boys up to?' With Dad, it was all a little more laissez-faire. I remember him padding down the stairs at three in the morning one Saturday to find me and a couple of buddies making pancakes in the kitchen. 'What the bloody hell are you doing?' he demanded.

'Er, making pancakes.'

He shrugged. 'Okay,' he said. Then he smiled and trudged back up to bed.

My parents' divorce didn't upset me like it might upset some other kids. I didn't want them to be living together and suffering just because they thought it was the right thing for me. If they were happier apart, that made perfect sense to me. Even when Mum and I moved from Redleaf, the only home I'd ever known, to a much smaller house on a nearby council estate, I remember being glad that she seemed happier. And when she softened the blow of moving house by agreeing that we could get Sky TV, I was made up. It's amazing what seems important to you when you're a kid.

My dad was, I think it's fair to say, suspicious about my early involvement in the film industry. He wasn't particularly worried about child fame, but I think he did have a concern that I might not be spending enough time with ordinary people, or Muggles, for want of a better word. I can understand his suspicion. He had worked incredibly hard to get where he was. He had four kids by the age of twenty-six. He knew the value of a pound and he was, I think, very concerned that his sons should, too. He wanted us to learn and emulate his incredibly strong work ethic. It must have been strange for him when I started earning money of my own from acting at an early age without having to work for it as hard as he did. Perhaps he was robbed of his paternal role. In a situation like that, it would be only natural that one might take a step back.

Sometimes that manifested itself in ways I found difficult to take. At the premiere of the fourth Potter film, when I had my mum and dad sitting either side of me, he teased me when the credits started rolling by saying: 'Well, you weren't in it much, were you?' His lack of enthusiasm seemed harsh at the time, but with the benefit of hindsight I find myself reading it differently. I now know, from speaking to his friends and workmates, the way my dad talked about me when I wasn't there. I now know he was very proud of me. I also now know that it's a classic British male trait, that reluctance to express emotion and say what you really think. I don't believe for a moment that my dad's suspicion of the film business meant that he didn't feel proud or care about me then. I think he just didn't know how to say it. He was trying to figure out a peculiar situation, and it can't have been easy.

My acting gave me an unusual degree of independence as a child, but Dad was also instrumental in developing that side of me. When I was nine he took me with him on a work trip to Amsterdam. I remember him sitting down outside a café in a big square and saying to me, 'Go on then, off you go.' I had no money and I didn't really know where I was, but he was insistent that I should be encouraged to figure stuff out for myself. At the time it seemed like indifference, but now I understand that it was a crucial part of my development. He knew that I might get lost, but if so I'd find my way back eventually. I might walk into a sex museum and be immediately kicked out, but with no harm done. I might fall on my face, but if so I'd learn how to get back up. All these would be important lessons. There would be times later in my life when I *would* fall on my face and I *would* have to get back up. I'm very grateful to my dad for that early instruction, and for everything else he did for me.

In the years that followed, I would find myself part of a different family. A wizarding family. My Muggle family, though, was like most families: loving, complex, occasionally flawed but always there for me. And beyond the basketballs and buffoonery, they went out of their way to provide me with the one thing I might easily have lacked as my life took an unusual turn: they provided me with a healthy dose of normality.

3

EARLY AUDITIONS

or

MOTHER GOOSE!

I became Draco Malfoy because my mum had a piece of glass in her foot.

Let me explain.

I was no child prodigy. Sure, I learned from my older brother Jink that it was okay to be interested in creative pursuits of all kinds. Sure, my mum was always supportive of whatever grabbed my fancy at any given moment. But I was born enthusiastic rather than talented.

This is not false modesty. I *did* have some ability as a singer. All four Felton brothers sang in the church choir at St Nick's in Bookham (although in the interest of full disclosure I should state that Chris was kicked out for pinching sweets from the tuck shop). And a prestigious choir school invited me to join, angelic little chap that I was, although as soon as they made me the offer I burst into tears because I didn't want to change school and leave my friends. Mum, characteristically, told me not to worry about it - but she does from time to time like to bring up the fact that I was accepted. That's mums for you. So the first time I remember being front and centre was not because of my acting. It was singing the solo in 'O Little Town of Bethlehem' one Christmas at St Nick's.

In addition to my choral exploits, I also went to an after-school drama club at the nearby Fetcham Village Hall. It took place every Wednesday afternoon: fifteen or twenty kids between the ages of six and ten, all chaotically putting on a play every three months for the mums and dads. Nothing serious, just little ones having fun. And it's worth repeating: I was nothing to write home about. I definitely wanted to go to the drama club, but my overriding memory of the performances is of embarrassment rather than glory. For one production - it might have been *A Christmas Carol* - I was given the artistically fulfilling and technically arduous role of 'Snowman Number Three'. My mum and granny went to great lengths to make me a snowman outfit, which comprised two wired dresses - one for my body, one for my head. It was an absolute nightmare to put on, and I still remember the ignominy of standing in the wings and peering out through a gap in the curtain to see three or four boys sniggering at the sight of little Tom Felton standing there butt naked, arms in the air, as they dressed me up in my snowman regalia. I've grown used to being frequently photographed, but I'm thankful that no photographic evidence exists of that particular moment.

On another occasion we staged *Bugsy Malone*. Off the back of my Oscar-worthy snowman performance I was promoted to 'Tree Number One'. The principal roles were given to the older children who crucially had the ability to speak coherently. I was one of the younger ones trusted with only a single line, rigorously committed to memory, assiduously rehearsed. I stood in line on the makeshift stage, patiently waiting for my cue.

And waiting.

And waiting.

Rehearsing my line in my head.

Preparing myself for my moment of glory.

And then, suddenly, I became aware of an excruciating silence. Everybody was looking expectantly at me. It was my moment and my mind was blank. And so I did what any self-respecting young actor would do: I burst into tears and waddled off the stage as fast as my branches would allow. After the show I ran to my mum, full of tears and apologies. *I'm so sorry, Mum. I'm so sorry!* My mum comforted me, told me it didn't matter, that it hadn't made the slightest difference to the story. But to this day I can still feel the shame. I'd let the team down!

In short, my acting career did not have the most auspicious start. I enjoyed it well enough, but I didn't excel. Then I started to get more homework, and my short-lived passion for learning the violin kicked in. I told Mum I didn't think I had time for the drama club any more, and that was that.

Except, that wasn't that.

The lady who ran the club was a very passionate, dramatic lady called Anne. When my mum told her that I was going to quit the drama club, her response was characteristically flamboyant: 'No, no, no! This child *belongs* in the arts! You must *promise* me that you'll take him to London to get an agent. He has *raw talent*! It would be a *terrible* waste if he does nothing with it!'

I'm absolutely certain she said this to lots of kids who left her club. I'd shown no special talent on those Wednesdays after school. Quite the opposite. This was surely just the melodramatic pronouncement of a theatrical lady. But she was persistent and her words planted a seed in my mind. Maybe I *could* get myself an acting agent. That would be pretty cool, no? Maybe the world of acting held more for me than the roles of Snowman Three and Tree One. I started to pester my mum to do just what Anne had suggested: to take me up to London to audition for an acting agency.

Mum was a busy lady, what with all those extra jobs she worked to keep us kids supplied with basketballs, fishing reels and violins. Ordinarily, she would never have been able to juggle all that and have time to take me on the train up to town to satisfy a whim like this, but that's where the piece of glass came in. It had been embedded in her foot for ages, but like most mums she just got on with life, putting her own needs second. The time came, however, that she had to have it dealt with. The shard was removed and she was on crutches for a few days. Significantly for me, it meant her having a week off work. So, with my pestering ringing in one ear and Anne's persuasiveness ringing in the other, she suggested that we make the trip to London.

We took the train from Leatherhead, Mum with her trusty *A to Z* in one hand and a crutch in the other. Our destination was the Abacus Agency, a tiny office up three flights of stairs somewhere in the middle of London. I felt pretty plucky as I said hello, introduced myself and took a seat. I had three big brothers, remember. It teaches you how to talk to people older than yourself. The process of auditioning, or so it seemed to me at the time, was simply to ensure that you weren't a complete spanner, or cripplingly camera shy. They gave me some paragraphs to read from *The Lion, the Witch and the Wardrobe*, and verified that far from being shy of the camera, all I wanted to do was fiddle with it and learn how it worked. They took a photograph of me to put into *Spotlight,* a kind of actors' catalogue, and packed me off home. I did nothing more than I imagine scores of kids did every week, but I must have done something right because a couple of weeks later the phone rang. It was the Abacus Agency offering me the opportunity to shoot a commercial in America.

You always remember the phone calls - the tingle of excitement when you hear that you've got the job. That first time was no exception. I was barely seven years old and they were giving me the chance to go to America, which none of us Felton boys had ever done. Not only was I heading on a two-week trip to the States, I was heading on a two-week trip to all the best bits of the States. The job was for an insurance company called Commercial Union, and the theme of the advert was 'invest with us and when you're an old man you can take your grandson on the road trip of a lifetime'. They needed to hire a cute kid to be the grandson, to stand in the right place holding his grandfather's hand at all the coolest locations in America, absolutely no talent required. Enter Tom.

My mum accompanied me, of course. We travelled to Los Angeles, Arizona, Las Vegas, Miami and New York. They put us up in hotels, quite a novelty for us. Mum was always particularly pleased if we stayed somewhere with a pool table, because that kept me quiet for hours, and I was transfixed by a thing of beauty called the Cartoon Network - another novelty - which meant I could watch cartoons *all day long*. I also discovered for the first time that certain hotels had a special system: you pick up the phone, call someone downstairs and they'll bring you food! In my case: French fries! I remember my mum timidly calling the producers and asking if it was okay to order me some fries and put it on the hotel bill. I imagine she was a refreshing change from the child-star tiger mums they were used to dealing with. We had no outrageous requests. I was perfectly happy sitting in my room watching *Johnny Bravo* with a plate of chips.

Our first day of filming took place in Times Square, perhaps Manhattan's busiest tourist trap and a big old leap from leafy Surrey and the Fetcham Village Hall. Barriers separated the film crew from the crowds and the traffic. There were people to do my hair, make-up and costume. I stood there wearing the beanie hat and big red puffa jacket that comprised my outfit and gradually became aware of people waving and cheering. I turned to look at them and realised that they were cheering at me! I grinned and waved back enthusiastically and they cheered some more. This was pretty fun. I was famous already! Brilliant! Except of course, I wasn't famous. I was entirely unknown. Turns out that with my angelic little face, my beanie and my puffa jacket they thought I was Macaulay Culkin in full *Home Alone* garb, or maybe his little brother. Sorry, Macaulay, for stealing your fans, even if it was just for one day.

I didn't mind. This was exciting and new and I had a taste for it. And there was something prescient about being mistaken for Macaulay Culkin, who was cast in *Home Alone* by the director Chris Columbus, because it was Chris who would go on to cast me as Draco Malfoy in the Harry Potter films.

I was paid the princely sum of £200 for that first advert, but I was too young to have much sense of what that meant. I was still happy with my twenty pence at the Dorking car boot sale, don't forget, and I was far more excited by the shiny red puffa jacket that they let me keep. I loved that puffa jacket. I was buzzing from the experience, though, and keen to tell everybody all about it. I used to go to a kids' club at Leatherhead Leisure Centre called Crazy Tots and I couldn't wait to share my adventures with my friends there. I didn't try to tell them about the Golden Gate Bridge or Caesars Palace or Times Square. I wanted to tell them about the *important* stuff: the room service, the Cartoon Network and, yes, the red puffa jacket. Pretty quickly, however, a hard truth presented itself.

Literally.

Nobody.

Cared.

I suppose the world I was trying to describe was so detached from Crazy Tots at the leisure centre that it was impossible for my friends to understand what I was on about. I soon learned to keep my trap shut.

I carried on auditioning. Auditions as an adult can be a pretty brutal experience, and believe me I've had my share. The bad ones aren't those when you walk into the audition room and can't stop farting (yes, it's happened). The bad ones are those when you realise that the person making the decision hasn't looked you in the eye from the moment you entered. The bad ones are those when there's a dancing bit in the middle that *you* know you can't do, and *they* know you can't do, and it's all going to be mortifying for everybody involved. As a kid, though, I rather took auditions in my stride, even the awful ones. I remember a particularly embarrassing casting call for a spaghetti commercial when I had to pretend to be an Italian kid and eata-a-bowla-pasta, cry 'mamma mia' and sing a little song. I didn't even like pasta at the time and I've no doubt that I looked daft as a doorknob. It didn't put me off. Mum managed to make our audition trips to London something of a treat. I'd do my bit, then we'd go to Hamleys, the toy shop on Regent Street, where I was allowed to play on the arcade machines in the basement while Mum had a cup of tea. And, of course, we both knew what might lie in store if I was successful. Another trip somewhere cool, another opportunity to binge-watch cartoons and order room service, and a £200 cheque at the end of it? Duh! Yes please!

It's always been the strange auditions that have got me the parts. That was certainly the case for my next job: a commercial for Barclaycard. It was a particularly exciting prospect for me because the face of Barclaycard at the time was my absolute favourite actor, the one I watched most as a youngster and who I completely fell in love with: Rowan Atkinson. Some of our happiest times as a family were when we sat all together in front of the TV watching *Mr Bean*. My dad would be pissing himself with laughter. My mum would try very hard not to snigger, usually unsuccessfully. We four boys would literally be in tears. So the opportunity to meet my hero - let alone appear alongside him - was incredibly exciting.

They were auditioning in pairs, so I found myself alongside a young girl in front of three or four casting executives. The girl had huge hair and was wearing a very colourful dress. 'There's no script,' they told us. 'When we say so, we want you both to mime as if you've just heard the doorbell and you're opening up the door and Mr Bean is standing there. You think you can do that?'

I nodded. I'd been through quite a few auditions by this time so I wasn't too nervous. The girl, though, seemed kind of kooky. She turned to the casting people and said: 'Are we allowed to faint?'

There was a moment. The casting people exchanged a look. I found myself thinking: wow, she's really going for it. Maybe I need to up my game.

'I think we'd rather you *didn't* faint,' one of them said.

She looked a bit crestfallen, but she nodded and the scene started. We both mimed opening up the door and then, before I could react at all and at the very top of her voice, the kooky girl inexplicably screamed: 'MOTHER GOOSE!' And she hit the floor like a toppled tree.

Silence. The casting people studiously avoided catching each other's eye. Obviously they couldn't laugh. I completely forgot I was supposed to be reacting to Mr Bean and just stared at the girl in astonishment. It was that reaction, I think, that got me the part, and I learned something from the experience: don't go into an audition with too much pre-planned. It's never about learning lines or whether you can cry on demand. It's about what's next, not what's now. Just react to what's around you. That girl, I think, had decided long before she entered the audition room that she was going to hit the deck, and it did her no favours.

Sadly for me, Rowan Atkinson pulled out of the Barclaycard campaign before shooting started, so I never did get to act with him. Mum and I had a pleasant enough jaunt around France filming the commercial, but I won't lie, it would have been a lot more fun if we'd had Mr Bean as a co-worker. I did get to go skiing, though. Sort of. One scene had me standing in skis at the top of a nursery slope. It was the first time I'd ever been in the mountains or seen that amount of snow. I was desperate to give skiing a go, but I was told in no uncertain terms that I wasn't to move a muscle. The last thing they wanted was a young actor with his leg in traction. Insurance wouldn't cover it. I did as I was told but the time would come, a few years down the line, when I would be somewhat less obedient when it came to observing the rules and regulations of a film set ...

4

THE MAGIC IN THE MAKING

or

JAMES BLOND AND THE GINGER WHISKER

My first on-screen enemy was a Potter, but not Harry. It was the nefarious lawyer Ocious P. Potter in the big-screen adaptation of the classic children's book *The Borrowers*. It's the story of a family of thumb-sized people living with - and hiding from - the life-sized 'human beans'. The youngest of the family is a cheeky little chap called Peagreen, for whom a cheeky little child actor was required. Enter nine-year-old Tom. I was, it's fair to say, a naughty fellow. If a whoopee cushion had found its way onto the teacher's chair, or they'd been locked out of their own classroom, there was a reasonable chance that I was involved in some way. I was young enough at the time for this to be cute and disarming - that wouldn't last for long - and it meant that I was well suited to the part of Peagreen.

I've only the sketchiest memories of auditioning for the part, though I do remember reading with the wonderful Flora Newbigin, who had already been cast as my older sister Arrietty, to see if the chemistry was right. A much clearer memory is of the joy of being released from school in order to go to rehearsals and filming. This was a different level of activity to the commercials I'd done previously. For those jobs, I'd simply be told where to stand and where to look. My input was minimal. *The Borrowers* was a real acting gig. Not only did I have a proper part to play, I also had stunts to do and so, during the pre-production period, my mum would pick me up from school at one o'clock every Monday, Wednesday and Friday. We had a driver called Jim, and our first stop would be to the local fish and chip shop. I'd choose a jumbo sausage and chips, which I'd eat in the car on the way to stunt training, with my mum furiously apologising all the way to Jim for stinking out his car with my lunch.

Those afternoon sessions took place in a vast gym where Olympic athletes trained. At the time I was all about James Bond, and I was a *little* disappointed that my stunt training didn't involve throwing myself from a moving car with a Walther PPK. It was fun, though. And compared to algebra classes, it was a dream come true. We learned basic gymnastics, we learned how to climb ropes using your legs rather than your hands, we learned how to fall from a height without shattering your ankles, we learned how to swing the hoops, jump on the mats and balance on the gymnastics beams. I was relatively physically able - hardly captain of the football team but decent enough with a cricket bat in hand - and so the stunt training wasn't too much of a physical challenge. My Peagreen-like cheekiness, however, presented more of a problem. I was walking along a beam one afternoon and decided it would be a very cool move to jump off the beam and land with my feet on either side. From up there, where I was standing, the levels looked about right and I didn't want to squander this opportunity to show off without people looking. So I shouted at everyone to stop what they were doing and watch me. They all turned to look. I gave them my best Billy Elliot pose, leaped into the air and parted my legs ready for my triumphant landing ...

Perhaps you can see where this story is heading? Suffice to say that my toes didn't hit the ground and my fall was broken by another, more sensitive part of my anatomy. The moment of impact was agonising and embarrassing in equal measure. My eyes water just to recall it. No doubt they watered then, too, but I remember doing my very best to keep it cool as a horrified silence fell over the gym and I shuffled off the beam, pretended that my stunt had gone *exactly* as I intended, and ran off to double over in private agony and nurse my wounded pride and my wounded ... well, I'll leave that to your imagination.

My pride would take another hit when the time came for the hair and make-up team to turn me into Peagreen. I can measure my childhood acting career by unusual haircuts. Long before Draco's bleached locks became a permanent feature of my life, I proudly sported Peagreen's quite ridiculous hairdo, a huge mass of orange curls - think Krusty the Clown, but ginger. If you think that's unappealing, you haven't heard the half of it. My wig only reached from the front of my hairline to the crown. This meant that the back of my head was entirely exposed. The only solution was to dye the back of it ginger, and perm it so that it curled. The net result was a tightly coiled orange mullet.

Reader, I ask you to contain yourself.

I was a keen footballer at the time. A life-sized cutout of Steve McManaman adorned my *Borrowers* dressing room, and like every self-respecting nine-year-old boy I collected football stickers. My heart's dearest desire was to move from the B team to the A team of my local football club, but because of filming, I missed a lot of practice sessions. When I could make it, I used to overcompensate to show them that I was worthy of the team. But it's difficult to look tough on the football pitch when you're sporting a curly orange mullet behind straight blond hair. Even our coach took the piss. 'You nearly had it by a hair's length, boys,' he told us after we'd narrowly lost a game. 'Or in Tom's case, a ginger whisker.' Everybody burst out laughing, including him. I saw the funny side and smiled sheepishly but alas, promotion to the A team eluded me.

I had no real sense as a kid that spending time on a film set was anything out of the ordinary. More than once I had to beg my mum to let me finish a game of footy when she was hassling me to get in the car and go to the studio. That said, filming *The Borrowers* was a pretty cool way to spend time as a kid. I loved getting kitted out in my wardrobe - dress a nine-year-old in an oversized sock and paperclip with a pair of thimbles as shoes and you're pretty much giving him the ultimate dress-up party. It certainly far surpassed my Snowman Number Three costume. More than that, though, I loved the set. There was a certain amount of green-screen visual effects work, but that technology was in its infancy and in order to establish the tininess of the Borrowers, everything on set had to be blown up to the most ridiculous scale. I spent my days strapped to harnesses, running along the insides of walls while enormous hammers smashed down at me. It was like being in my very own video game. For one scene, I had to be trapped inside a milk bottle as high as a bus is long, which they filled up with a thick, stinky white liquid to approximate milk. It was a huge stunt that we spent days on. For another, I had to hold on to a pole thirty feet in the air before falling onto a huge crash mat. Nowadays, I'd be a terrified mess before trying a stunt like that. Back then, I insisted on doing it several times - just to ensure my performance was up to scratch, you understand. Can a kid have much more fun than that? I'm not sure how.

But perhaps even more exciting than filming inside my own personal Super Mario world was that we were based at Shepperton Studios. And what else should be filming there at the same time but the new James Bond film, *Tomorrow Never Dies*. This, for me, was a Very Big Deal. I changed the name on my dressing room from 'Peagreen' to 'The Next James Bond' and I was stoked that some of the stunt crew from *GoldenEye* were working with me on *The Borrowers*. Shepperton is a series of massive empty warehouses where they build whatever sets they need. To go from A to B you take a little electric golf buggy. It's a blast because on any given day you might drive past a fully made-up pirate eating a sandwich, or an alien having a sneaky cigarette. For me it was extra thrilling because there would routinely be several James Bonds milling around the studios. They were stunt doubles and stand-ins in their sharp suits and dark wigs, but from the back they were Bond, and that was good enough for me. But just once, sitting in the back of the buggy as we trundled across the studios, I did a double take. The Bond we had just passed was no stunt double. It was Pierce Brosnan himself, the real deal. We didn't exchange any words. I don't think we even exchanged a glance. All the same, that was one of the most exciting moments of my life so far. And while my friends weren't that interested in my life on set, my brush with Bond was a pretty cool story to tell.

Of course, *The Borrowers* had its own cast of heavy-weights, not that I was old enough to realise it at the time. John Goodman was a prestigious actor with a commanding presence. I remember one day running around the hair and make-up rooms with a Super Soaker water gun, and I burst like Bond into one of the rooms, full of giggles and trouble, where John was quietly having his make-up done. He silenced me with a single, stern look in the mirror. A look that said: let's not screw around here, kid. It was enough to make me dash out again, no word spoken. My mum was particularly thrilled to meet my on-screen mother, Celia Imrie, one of her personal heroes because of her work with Victoria Wood. Mum's excitement rubbed off on me, but really I had no idea who she was. All I know is that she was instrumental in creating a relaxed atmosphere on set so that we kids didn't feel in any way under pressure. As soon as you shout at a child on set, chances are they won't be coming out of their shell any time soon. Celia's fun, motherly nature made sure that didn't happen.

And although I didn't know it at the time, I was to have my first introduction to the Harry Potter family. Jim Broadbent, who played my dad, would go on to play the bumbling Professor Slughorn. Jim was a lovely guy through and through: a great sense of humour, quietly spoken but brilliant at funny voices, and always supportive to us kids. I would also meet Mark Williams, who went on to play Arthur Weasley. He was playful - childish almost - and though we didn't film any scenes together, he was a lot of fun to be around. I definitely don't think he would have disapproved of me jumping in with a Super Soaker. He'd have been more likely to join in. Thanks to the disarming, relaxing presence of Celia, Jim and Mark, I never thought of taking anything too seriously.

They say you learn best when you're having fun. Almost without realising it, I started to do just that. I suppose, being surrounded by actors of a certain stature, it was inevitable that I should start to absorb something about the art of performance, and there's no doubt that *The Borrowers* required more of me than the commercials that preceded it. What I really remember learning, though, was the nitty-gritty technical business of how a film set works. It was basic stuff, but it would serve me well in my future career. I learned to put myself into the position of the camera operator, so if they told me to look camera left, I would have to look to my right. I learned to pay attention to the tiny chalk marks on the floor that told me where I could walk up to without forcing the focus puller to shift focus. Most importantly, I learned that when you hear those magic words 'Roll cameras', and the accelerating click of the film spool rotating, everyone on set has to be on the ball. In those days we were shooting on 35mm film, so every minute of shooting time was costing thousands of pounds.

Not that I was always a model of professionalism and restraint. When the teacher tells a certain kind of child to be quiet it can ignite a spark of naughtiness, and I probably had more of that particular spark than most. I had a tendency to dissolve into fits of laughter just before the camera rolled: everyone shouting 'Quiet!' was enough to set me off. In general, the adults took this in their stride. However, on one occasion I did receive the most restrained of bollockings. The director, Peter Hewitt - a thoroughly pleasant and patient chap - came up to me. To this day I can recall the look on his face: the pained expression of a man under immense pressure, with the clock ticking and camera film running out, having to find a way to coax a giggling nine-year-old out of his hysterics and into filming mode. Picture it.

INT. SHEPPERTON STUDIOS. DAY.

PETER

Tom, please, it's time to stop laughing.

Tom clamps his lips together. He nods. Then he starts laughing again.

PETER

(an edge of desperation in his voice)

No, Tom. Really. It's time to stop laughing.

Tom furrows his brow. Something in his expression tells us he just twigged that the director really means it. So he nods. Looks serious. Then starts laughing again.

Peter closes his eyes. Takes a deep a breath. Opens them. When he speaks again, it's with the expression of a deeply frustrated man doing his very best to keep calm.

PETER

Tom. Please. I'm not joking. You *have* to stop laughing.

And he gives Tom the hint of a smile that says: do we have a deal here?

We had a deal. I could tell I was being told off in the nicest possible way. The camera started rolling and I managed to pull myself together.

I wouldn't have had half as much fun, though, if it had been *all* adults. I remember being massively influenced by Flora. She was a few years older than me, but always a laugh and a pleasure to be around. Even though this was her first major film she definitely knew her way around the set and she held my hand, literally and metaphorically. She made sure I was standing on my mark, and my dodgy-looking wig wasn't askew. Thanks to her I had a brilliant time on *The Borrowers*. So much so that I cried when it was all over.

We had just wrapped the film. It was six o'clock in the evening and I was sitting in the make-up chair for the last time so that the make-up lady could cut out my orange perm. All of a sudden I felt overwhelmed with a confusing torrent of emotions that I couldn't understand. Tears welled in my eyes, but let's be honest, the future James Bond needs to be tough enough to keep his feelings in check. So I devised a cunning plan. I pretended that the poor make-up lady had nicked me with her scissors and howled, 'Ow! You got me!'

Alas, my cunning plan was more Baldrick than Blackadder. She hadn't got me. She hadn't even been near me and she told me so. But for the next hour I used my imaginary wound as an excuse for the tears that wouldn't stop.

I didn't appreciate it in that moment, but my tears were teaching me another important lesson. An audience can go back and watch a film any number of times they want. It's always there for them. For the cast and crew, the relationship with a film is more complex. The magic is in the making, and that process is a discreet unit of time in the past. You can reflect on that unit of time, you can be proud of it, but you can't revisit it. If shooting *The Borrowers* had been like living in my own personal Super Mario game, reaching the end was like coming to a checkpoint. I could look back, but I knew I'd never live that part of my life again. In the years to come, that feeling would return at the end of every shoot. For months, you've been a travelling circus act. You've been a tight-knit community. You've travelled to a dozen different cities. You've broken bread together. You've acted together. You've messed up together and got it right together. You've left your home and your families, you've bundled up together in a hotel miles away, and while it's not always jokes and laughter, you develop a certain bond and intimacy. And then, suddenly, it's over, and this community that has been your surrogate family dissipates to the four corners of the earth. It doesn't exist anymore. We almost always say the same thing: that we'll be in touch, that we'll hook up next week, that we'll relive the old times, and no doubt we mean it sincerely. Occasionally it does even happen. We all know, though, deep down, that we've reached the checkpoint. Whatever your experience on the film, good or bad, a moment in time that was special and unique has passed and we can never get it back. In the years to come I learned that this would not get any easier, especially on a project the size of Harry Potter.

The nine-year-old Tom could only fumble at the edges of these emotions. The nine-year-old Tom knew nothing of the passing of time. He was more interested in getting back to the football pitch or the carp lake than analysing his feelings in any depth. But as he sat in that make-up chair having his ginger mullet cut away, perhaps he sensed for the first time the loss of something precious.

It was a taste of things to come, because the thirty-something Tom still bawls his eyes out every time a job comes to an end.

5

MY BROTHERS ARE ALREADY SICK OF IT

or

PROJECTILES AT THE PREMIERE

You always remember your first time. Thanks to my brothers, I certainly will.

The premiere of *The Borrowers,* at the Odeon Leicester Square, was not my first screening of the film. That happened at a screening room at the Hard Rock Café, a treat laid on by the filmmakers for me and some school friends. It's a happy memory and I think my friends enjoyed it, but that might have had something to do with the free mini-burgers and Coke. The premiere itself was an altogether more elaborate affair. It was nothing on the level of what was to come, but it was still a big deal. None of my family had ever been to a film premiere before, so we didn't know what to expect and Mum and Dad couldn't prepare me for the experience. There were crowds outside and this time they weren't cheering for Macaulay Culkin, they were cheering for me and the rest of the cast. I don't think, though, that I let it go to my head too much. Did I mention that having three older brothers tends to keep you grounded?

We arrived in a convoy of Morris Minors - the classic cars that were used in the film - and I stepped outside in my snazzy white suit, black tie and white shirt (I told you I had an early eye on the James Bond gig). It was a little intimidating, so I stuck close to Flora. She was my safety net. She carried a lot more of the weight of the film on her shoulders than I did. She was Batman, I was Robin. She was Harry, I was Ron (almost literally, with my orange hair). Flora was confident and articulate and incredibly good at dealing with the cameras and the interviews. I stuck close and followed her eloquent lead.

While I was outside doing the red carpet, my family headed into the cinema. Here they found lots of well-dressed, pretty ladies holding trays of free champagne. How did they know it was free? They each confirmed its price by asking the pretty ladies separately. My eldest brother Jink took particular advantage of the complimentary booze, as any self-respecting sixteen-year-old would have done. And since he had an hour to kill between our arrival and the start of the film, he had plenty of time in which to do it. He surreptitiously necked several glasses and, when the time came, made his unsteady way into the auditorium. The opening credits hadn't even started to roll, however, when Jink felt a sudden, urgent need to be elsewhere. He stood up, stumbled past a few irritated audience members in his aisle, and disappeared.

Five minutes passed. No sign of Jink. My dad muttered a few choice words and went off to find his wayward eldest son. Predictably enough, he was locked in a toilet cubicle on his knees, worshipping the porcelain as the free champagne worked its way back out. My dad stood outside the cubicle, suited and booted, while Jink heaved his guts out. And the icing on the cake? A punter wandered in and, seeing him standing there in his suit, mistook my dad for a toilet attendant and tipped him a pound. It was not, all in all, how he expected his evening to pan out (but he did keep the pound).

So Jink missed the film, my dad missed the film and the evening's festivities weren't over yet. A huge after-party followed. It was held in a massive warehouse dressed with the oversized props from the film, with music, games, sweets and - you guessed it - more free champagne. This time it was the turn of Ash - aged thirteen and following in his older brother's footsteps - to sample the fruits of the French countryside. With several glasses down his gullet, he decided it would be a good idea to have a go on the enormous bouncy castle with Chris. It was *not* a good idea. The bouncy castle was being used by kids half their age and size. Chris accidentally kneed a nine-year-old in the back of the head. Not to be outdone by his older brother, Ash took a few bounces and then projectile vomited in spectacular fashion into the corner of the castle. He crawled off the castle, belched loudly and announced, 'I feel much better now!'

All in all, I think it's fair to say that the behaviour of the Felton brothers that evening was, at best, mixed. But I didn't let it upset me. I just enjoyed the evening for what it was. After all, it wasn't like I had any big hopes of being an actor or, even more unlikely, a movie star. I'd had my moment in the sun and the chances were that this would be my first and last film premiere. Wouldn't it?

6

ANNA AND THE KING

or

CLARICE AND HANNIBAL

I won't lie. Although I'd never really considered myself to have any special acting talent - and I had no sense that I'd fulfilled the prophecy of Anne from the drama club - I did feel satisfied with *The Borrowers*. I thought I was okay in it. It was fun to watch myself on the big screen. Perhaps that was terrible arrogance. Or perhaps it meant I was free from the self-awareness and self-criticism of an adult.

I love to visit the theatre. I go for the performance, of course, but I also go to experience the reactions of an audience to a work of art. One of the most moving responses I ever saw was at the musical *Matilda*, where I sat near a little boy no more than five years old who was there with his mum. He couldn't take his eyes off the stage. No doubt he could barely follow the story. I'm sure many of the jokes went over his head. He was simply lost in the experience. For me, it was a bit of a tear-jerker. It would have made no sense to ask him if he *liked* the show or not. He was too young to be a critic and it reminded me of that time before I had succumbed to the adult tyranny of judgement and self-consciousness.

Now, whenever anybody asks me about acting, my advice is always the same. Be playful. Childlike, even. Separate yourself from the tedious analysis of adults. Forget about good and bad. It's a mantra that serves me well. I often try to force myself to be more like the young Tom in *The Borrowers,* or that little boy watching *Matilda,* free from the crippling restriction of self-consciousness.

Some of that freedom was still with me when I auditioned for my next big film. *Anna and the King* was a step up from *The Borrowers* in terms of scale and prestige. Jodie Foster - a huge Hollywood star - was cast in the lead role, and filming would take place over a period of four months in Malaysia. The casting process was much more rigorous than anything I'd encountered before. I attended two or three auditions in London and then, once I was down to the last two, I travelled to Los Angeles for a final audition.

The hindsight of an adult tells me this was a special moment. But I was still a child, and I had no sense of this being anything massively out of the ordinary. They flew my mum and me to Los Angeles and we were put up in a crazy huge hotel, which to my absolute delight had not only an indoor swimming pool but also a jacuzzi. What kid doesn't love a jacuzzi? What kid doesn't hilariously pretend it's an enormous farting cauldron? Or was that just me? I was far more interested in re-acquainting myself with room service and the Cartoon Network than in the audition. My recollection is that the other boy who was up for the part had a much more hands-on mum than mine. She was reading lines with him, almost directing him. My mum never did anything like that. She never tried to train me, never told me how to say something, always encouraged me to trust my instincts. In many ways I was completely unprepared, but it was that attitude, I think, that won me the part. Remember the Mother Goose girl? I was once again the complete opposite. I walked into that Hollywood audition free of any anxiety or preconceptions. I was just normal Tom and I think that's what they were looking for. They wanted to see that I was happy with twelve people watching me, clutching notepads, whispering in each other's ears, because if I wasn't happy with that, I wouldn't be comfortable on a film set. They wanted to see that I was malleable and directable. They wanted to see that I could deliver a line in more than one way. Most of all, I think they wanted to see that I was relaxed, and I think I was helped more than anything else by the fact that I wanted the interview to be over so I could get back to the hotel and its hilarious farting cauldron.

Mum and I returned home to Surrey and I didn't think too much more about the film. I was still more interested in getting into the A team for football. Maybe I had a better chance, now that my haircut was a bit more streamlined. A few weeks later, though, Mum picked me up from school and, walking back to the car, she said she had news: 'You got the part!'

I felt a surge of excitement. 'Really?'

'Really.'

I felt a surge of hunger. 'Did you bring me a cheese straw, Mum?'

I was obsessed with cheese straws. Still am. Far more so than making films.

The decision was made: Mum and I were off to Malaysia for four months. I'd barely heard of Malaysia, and none of my family had even been to Asia. We had no idea what to expect, but we were both very excited. Mum quit her job and off we went.

It would have been a lonely four months without my mum. It was the first time that I had separated myself from the normality of a day at school with my friends, and I missed it. There was no social media back in those days. I certainly didn't have a mobile phone. I don't think I spoke to any of my friends more than once or twice during the whole four months. My dad and brothers came to visit only once, for a week. I was the only Western child on set, which was a little disorientating, but I quickly made friends with the locals.

I also had my first experience of one-on-one tutoring, which took place for three to six hours a day in a cold, draughty Portakabin with one tiny window. And although my private tutor, Janet, was a lovely and intelligent lady, I missed the bustle of the classroom, the proximity of my mates and, yes, the opportunity to play up. It's hard to be the class clown in a class of one. On-set tutoring would be a feature of my life throughout my childhood and I'm afraid I never grew to love it. My obsession at the time was rollerblading. When I wasn't filming or in lessons, I would nag my mum to take pictures of me doing fake grinds and tricks on my rollerblades so I could send them back to my mates and show them what a cool time I was having. But I don't think I fooled anyone.

I might have sometimes been lonely out in Malaysia, but I did meet new people from different walks of life, and I can't overstate how much that kind of cultural enrichment helped me later in life. My mum went out of her way to make the experience easier for me. The film's budget was enormous, which meant that the catering was on another level. They served incredible five-star meals in a huge marquee comprising pan-seared this and truffled that. I wouldn't touch any of it. I had, and still have, very plain tastes in food and not much of an appetite. I was more than happy with a chocolate bar and a bag of crisps rather than any of the fancy food on offer. In an attempt to get me to eat something other than sweets, Mum would venture out in the car to find me my favourite chicken nuggets from KFC. She doesn't much like driving round the quiet lanes of Surrey, let alone the busy highways of central Kuala Lumpur, but she braved them. Thanks to her, I was spared a nasty bout of food poisoning that knocked the rest of the cast and crew out for a week. So don't tell me that chicken nuggets are always bad for you.

Like any kid, I had my off days, when the homesickness and the isolation got too much. I remember a handful of mornings spent crying, wailing that I didn't want to do it anymore. I remember sweating my butt off in a six-piece linen suit that took an hour to put on and take off. I remember tearfully begging to be allowed to go home. But then by the afternoon I'd have calmed down and everything would be okay again.

And, of course, there was Jodie Foster.

My brothers had been trying to get me to watch *Silence of the Lambs* for years, but my mum had rightly shut the door on their attempts to scare the living daylights out of me (although they still managed to sneak in a viewing of *Terminator 2*). So I had no real concept of quite how famous Jodie was. Of course, I was *told* that she was very important, so I might have been forgiven for thinking she was more in the John Goodman mould than the Mark Williams mould. If I thought that, I was wrong. Jodie Foster couldn't have been lovelier. I would grow to learn that, on a film set, everything trickles down from the top. If the actor whose name is at the top of the call sheet is difficult, the whole shoot becomes difficult. Jodie Foster - and her co-star Chow Yun-Fat - exhibited kindness, politeness, patience and, most importantly, enthusiasm for the process. Jodie even managed to keep her cool when I kicked her hard in the face.

We were shooting at the time. Jodie played my mother, brought into the court of the king of Siam to provide a Western education for the harem and the children. My character Louis gets into an argument with another kid who pins him to the floor. Jodie has to come and separate us. I was blindly bicycle-kicking my legs when I clonked her straight in the mouth. It was not a glancing blow. It was a proper whack and I'm sure plenty of other actors would have had something to say about it. Not Jodie. She was perfectly lovely about the whole affair, even when the moment of impact was shown several times on the blooper reel at the wrap party.

• • •

Let me take you forwards several years. I'm in my twenties and an audition request comes in. It's for a film called *Hitchcock*, about the making of the film *Psycho*, and starring Sir Anthony Hopkins. So having done a film as a kid with Jodie Foster, it would be cool to get the *Silence of the Lambs* clean sweep and work with both of the leads, right?

Well, maybe not. The audition came up in the morning and I was called for that very afternoon. There was barely time to read the script, let alone research it. I was reading for the part of Anthony Perkins, who plays Norman Bates. I'd not seen the film, so I watched some footage of him and it quickly became apparent that I was uniquely unsuited for the part. He was nearly six foot two. I'm not. He had dark hair and dark eyes. I don't. He exuded a kind of psychopathic menace. I ... well, you can be the judge of that.

It was one of the few times that I've ever called my agent from my car outside the building and said, 'Do I *really* have to read for this? I just don't think I'm right for it. Perhaps the chance to work with Anthony Hopkins will come up another time, with a more suitable project.' They agreed, but persuaded me to turn up anyway, just to show my face to the director and producers.

So I turned up. I sat waiting outside the audition room. The door opened and out came the American actress Anna Faris, who had been auditioning before me. In an exaggerated stage whisper, she pointed back into the room and said, 'He's in there!'

Who's in there? She was gone before I could ask her.

I entered the audition room. As expected, I saw a line of producers, dressed sharply, along with the director.

As not expected, I also saw Sir Anthony Hopkins himself, casually dressed, sitting there ready to read with me. By this time I'd seen *Silence of the Lambs* several times. Now I was about to read a scene with Hannibal Lecter, completely unprepared.

My stomach turned over. I was bricking it, horribly aware that I didn't know the script, I didn't know the character, I knew nothing about the film and I didn't even think I should be here. But I was committed now. So we shook hands and I took a seat opposite him.

We get started. Sir Anthony reads the first line. I read my line in a very unimpressive American accent. He stares at me. He blinks. He smiles. He puts his script to one side and says, 'I'll tell you what, let's forget the script. Let's talk to you as the character. Let's find out if you really *know* this character.'

Know this character? I barely knew the character's name. I knew nothing about him. I was completely out of my depth.

'Okay,' I squeaked.

Sir Anthony fixed me with an intense stare. 'So tell me,' he said. 'Tell me what your character feels about ... *murder*?'

I stared back at him, trying to match his Hannibal Lecter-like intensity. And I said ... Well, I wish I could remember what I said. It was something so absurd, so traumatically cringe-worthy, that my brain has blocked it from my memory. He asked me more questions, each more peculiar than the last. What does your character feel about this? What does your character feel about that? My answers went from cringeworthy to downright bizarre. Until finally, he said, 'What does your character feel about ... children?'

'Children?'

'Children.'

'Er ...' I said.

'Yes?' said Sir Anthony.

'Um ...' I said.

'What does he *like*?' said Sir Anthony.

'He likes ... he likes ... children's *blood*,' I said.

Shocked silence. I looked at him. He looked at me. The producers looked at each other. I wanted to crawl into the corner and die.

Sir Anthony nodded. He cleared his throat and politely said, with the tiniest of smiles, 'Thanks for coming in.' And what he meant was: that was excruciating, please leave before you say anything worse.

The relief of leaving the building outweighed the skin-crawlingly poor performance with Sir Anthony. Not by much, but enough for me to excitedly call some of my mates to tell them the tale of the worst audition ever.

7

THE POTTER AUDITIONS

or

WHEN DRACO MET HERMIONE

Until the age of eleven, I attended a slightly posh private boys' school called Cranmore. It was no Hogwarts - forget about turrets and lakes and great halls. But it was a very academic place. A place where it was cool to be top of the class and you were respected for good grades rather than, say, bunking off to lark about on a film set. My grandfather helped fund my place. He was an academic - more about him later - and instead of saving up for a college fund, he helped put all four boys through early private education. The idea was to drill in some academia while we were young and impressionable.

If I have any academic abilities - basic arithmetic, the idea of reading being something enjoyable - they derive entirely from those years at Cranmore. By the time my stint at private school was almost up, however, my attention was beginning to wander. I distinctly remember, during my last couple of months, that there would be a half-hour period after lunch when the teacher would sometimes read us a story out loud. One day he chose some book about a boy wizard living under the stairs. Truth to tell, it wouldn't much have mattered what he was reading, I would have had the same reaction, which was: give it a rest, mate! A boy wizard? Not my cup of tea.

When I was eleven I changed school. My new school was closer to home and a good deal more down to earth. It was called Howard of Effingham, and if Cranmore taught me my three Rs, Howard taught me how to socialise with anyone and everyone. For the first time, I saw students talk back to teachers - practically unheard of at Cranmore. I saw kids smoking on school premises and girls being sent home because their skirts were too short. I had no idea what the future held for me, of course, but to this day I think my life could have been very different if I hadn't switched schools. Private schools and film sets are both out-of-the-ordinary environments. Howard of Effingham gave me a healthy dose of normality.

Not that the transition was easy. For the first week as a Year 7, everybody had to wear the uniform of whatever school they'd just come from. This meant most kids were in the same garb: a T-shirt and a pair of shorts. For me and only one other - my mate Stevie - it meant a maroon cap, a blazer and socks pulled up to my knees. In short, it meant looking like a complete spanner, and there was no shortage of people to tell me so. It didn't make for a straightforward introduction, but looking back I was glad of the change. I'd grown up thinking that the way to get on in the world was by being a brainbox. I was beginning to learn that a far more important and effective skill is the ability to communicate with people from all walks of life. Being placed in a more normal environment would help me do that. It would become even more of an advantage as other parts of my life became less than normal.

Up until that point I'd got away with being a cheeky little boy. In fact, I'd more than got away with it - it had landed me film roles. There comes a time, though, as adolescence hits, that cheekiness develops into something else. I became a bit of a pain in the arse. A bit of a reprobate. Don't get me wrong, I lived in a pleasant part of Surrey and as reprobates went, I was quite a posh one. Really, I was just doing my best to fit into my new environment. Just doing my best to be ordinary.

And I *was* ordinary. Sure, I had a bit of acting experience. I'd done some commercials and a couple of films. But nobody cared about that. My new friends were much more interested in skateboarding, amateur pyrotechnics and sharing a cigarette behind the bike sheds. I don't think *I* even really cared that much about filming. It was a fun sideline, but nothing more. I certainly had no intention for acting to become anything more serious. If I never appeared in another film again, that would be okay.

And maybe that would happen. I was developing a bit of a swagger. A slight arrogance. Surely nobody would want to give a part to a kid displaying those sorts of qualities, would they?

• • •

I had no idea, when I was first asked by my agents to audition for a film called *Harry Potter and the Philosopher's Stone*, that it would be any different in terms of scale to the jobs I'd done previously. In my mind it was another *Borrowers*: a relatively high-budget film with lots of children and, if I played my cards right, a part for me. But if I didn't get a part? That was okay too. It wasn't the be-all and end-all. There was a good chance something else would come along.

It soon became clear, however, from the auditioning process at least, that there were differences. These were open auditions. I'd been asked by my agents to go along but the vast majority of kids had turned up because they loved the Harry Potter books. I think I was perhaps the only kid at the whole audition who had no idea what they were or how much they meant to people. I'd certainly long forgotten those after-lunch story sessions about the boy wizard.

The auditioning process was longer and more drawn out than anything I'd experienced before. Sure, there were no trips to Hollywood, but the casting was distinctly more involved than usual. There were thousands of kids to audition. It took a long time to give each one their individual chance of success. It must have been exhausting for the casting team. I approached it with my usual lack of overt enthusiasm. Whereas all the other kids were wildly excited about the prospect of being in a film, and clearly knew the book inside out, I was the complete opposite.

They stood thirty of us in a line. One of the adults - I would later find out that this was the director, Chris Columbus - went down the line asking each of us which part of the book we were most excited to see on screen. I remember being underwhelmed by the question. As the responses came, clear and certain - Hagrid! Fang! Quidditch! - I remember standing there wondering if I could go home soon. It was only when it came to the turn of the kid next to me that I realised not only had I given the question zero thought, I had absolutely no idea what anybody was talking about. Who was Hagrid? What was a Quidditch? My neighbour announced that he was most excited to see Gringotts, and I thought to myself, *What the hell are they? Some kind of flying animal, maybe?*

There was no time to find out. Chris Columbus turned to me. 'What bit of the book are *you* most looking forward to seeing, Tom?'

I stalled. There was an awkward silence in the audition room. I gave my most winning smile and pointed at the Gringotts guy. 'Same as him, mate!' I said. I made a little flapping motion with my arms. 'Can't wait to see those Gringotts!'

There was a heavy pause.

'You mean you're looking forward to seeing Gringotts ... the bank?' Columbus said.

'Oh yeah,' I blagged quickly. 'The bank! Can't wait!'

He gave me a long look. He knew I was bullshitting. I knew he knew I was bullshitting. He nodded, then continued down the line to a flurry of enthusiastic and informed responses.

Ah well, I thought. *You win some, you lose some.*

But the audition wasn't over. Columbus announced that we were going to take a break. 'You guys just hang out here,' he said. 'Nobody's going to be filming you. Just do what you want to do.' It was, of course, a bit of a scam. The cameras were rolling and a huge fluffy boom mic hung over the room. I'd been on sets before, I could tell what was going on and I felt pretty cocky about it. I certainly didn't feel inclined to fall into their trap.

A young, curious girl approached me. She had brown frizzy hair and couldn't have been more than nine years old. She pointed at the boom mic. 'What's that?' she asked.

I glanced up at it, world-weary and slightly full of myself. I might even have sneered a little. 'What's what?'

'That?'

'It means they're recording us. Obviously.' I turned my back on her and wandered off, leaving the little girl to gaze wide-eyed around the room. I later found out that her name was Emma Watson. It was her first time in a film environment. I don't know whether anybody overheard our little exchange, but if they did, they'd definitely have seen a little Slytherin in me.

The final part of the audition was a one-on-one with Columbus on his own. It's hard to audition a kid; realistically, how good are they going to be if you simply hand them a monologue and give them the stage? Columbus had a talent, though, for bringing out what he wanted to see in us. We rehearsed a short scene where Harry is asking Hagrid about a dragon's egg. Real dragons' eggs being hard to come by, the prop was an ordinary chicken's egg. The scene was simple. We rehearsed it once and then they rolled cameras.

```
INT. AN AUDITION ROOM. DAY.

                    TOM
        (as Harry)
    What's that, Hagrid?

                  COLUMBUS
        (in best Hagrid voice)
    That's a very precious Norwegian
    Ridgeback egg, that is.
```

TOM

Wow! A real dragon's egg! Where did you get it?

COLUMBUS

They're very rare, these are, 'Arry. They're very hard to come by.

TOM

Can I hold it?

A beat.

COLUMBUS

Alright, but be careful mind – it's very fragile…

He delicately started to pass the egg towards me but, just as he was about to hand it over, he purposely dropped it. The egg smashed on the floor. Dragon everywhere. He watched for my reaction. I think most kids would have felt the need to say something, or would have been alarmed at the turn the scene had taken. I just giggled, little sod that I was.

My cheekiness - or cockiness, call it what you will - was evidently no barrier to progress. I was recalled several times after that first day. I read at least a couple of times for Harry, and also for Ron. This time round there were a few simple lines from the film, but they meant nothing to me as I still really had no idea who this wizard under the stairs was, or his ginger-haired mate. They gave me round glasses to wear, and put a scar on my forehead. I spent the entire day at the studio with others on the shortlist. At one stage they even dyed my hair Ron-coloured, though happily I avoided another permed ginger mullet. I started to entertain the idea that perhaps it would be pretty cool to play this Harry Potter kid ...

But then the auditions were over and I didn't hear anything for weeks.

Ah well. No news is good news, right?

Wrong.

Our yearly family holidays took place at Eurocamp in France. Mum, Dad and the four Felton boys would pile into our old blue Transit van that had a regular tendency to break down halfway along the autoroute. Those were the best holidays of my life, no question. Fresh baguettes. Discovering Nutella. I remember hanging out around the tents that summer, idly playing with my yoyo while my mum read the newspaper. She called me over to look at a photograph.

The picture showed two boys and a girl. One of the boys had dark hair. The other had a ginger mop. The girl had long brown frizzy hair and I immediately recognised her as the kid to whom I'd been less than charitable at the audition. The headline read: 'Harry Potter Cast Revealed'.

I made an outward show of nonchalance. 'Oh well,' I said. 'Next time.' And I wandered off to carry on playing with my yoyo. I won't lie, there was a twinge of disappointment. But I mastered it quickly and ten minutes later I'd moved on. Maybe it would have been fun to be a wizard, but it wasn't going to happen, so I might as well enjoy my holiday and play with my yoyo in the sunshine.

• • •

And then, of course, I was recalled. They didn't want me for Harry or Ron (or Hermione). They had another part in mind. Draco Malfoy, the bad guy. Apparently.

I'd like to tell you that the twelve-year-old Tom was inspired to squirrel himself away with some Harry Potter books as a result of being involved with the auditions, but he wasn't. It helped, I think. The filmmakers weren't so much looking for actors; they were looking for people who *were* these characters. With Daniel, Rupert and Emma, they nailed it. They pretty much *are* - or at least they were - Harry, Ron and Hermione. And while I like to think Draco and I were not *exactly* alike, there was surely something about my general nonchalance that caught the eye. Would Draco have gone home to mug up, Hermione-like, on Harry Potter books? I think not. Would he have blagged his way through a question about which character he was most excited to see on screen? Possibly.

You had to act the part, but more importantly you had to look the part. They decided that they needed to see what I looked like with white hair. It meant the first of the many bleachings that would become a staple in my life for the next ten years. It took a lot longer than I expected to establish my first ever Malfoy hairdo. You can't just go from one colour to another, especially when going lighter. It's a matter of applying layers of peroxide and then topping up with tint. The peroxide burned my head first time round. It felt like fire ants were nibbling at your scalp. Agony. Then they said they'd have to do it again and I begged them not to. My plea fell on deaf ears: I was straight back in the hairdresser's chair. It initially took six or seven rounds over a matter of days to achieve the colour. It was important for the filmmakers that the colouring was just right. They needed to see how the Malfoy blond looked next to the Weasley ginger or the Granger brown. I spent hours doing camera tests next to swatches of different colours to give them an idea of how I might look in dark Hogwarts robes, for example, or green and silver Slytherin Quidditch gear.

And they needed to know how I would appear on screen next to Harry, Ron and Hermione. The three principals were there for one of my last auditions so that they could see how our colouring, our heights and our general demeanours offset against each other. We'd reached the point in the audition process where we needed to read a scene together - there was no messing about with chicken eggs now - so we worked on Harry and Draco's first encounter.

I'm a year older than Rupert, two years older than Daniel and nearly three years older than Emma. As we moved through the films, that age difference became less important. But there's a big difference between a twelve-year-old and a nine-year-old and my recollection is that I did *feel* much older. These first moments were as awkward as any first meeting between kids. We were all quite shy (Rupert less so ...). Off camera, I was probably a little aloof towards these younger kids. I was the product of a family with three older brothers, remember, and more than a little of their adolescent standoffishness had rubbed off on me. No doubt some of that transferred to the camera tests. Would it help me get the part, though?

• • •

A week or two later, I was in the garden of my friend Richie's house, playing football. His mum Janice shouted out of the window, 'Tom, your mum's on the phone!'

I was a bit irritated. The game wasn't going my way. I ran into the house and impatiently picked up the phone, huffing and puffing. 'Yeah?'

'You got it!'

'What?'

'You got the part!'

'What part?'

'Draco!'

There was a moment of silence while I let it sink in.

'Cool,' I said. 'This should be fun.'

Then I said, 'Um, can I go now, Mum? I'm 2-1 down.'

I'd like to say there were fireworks, but really I just wanted to get back to the footy. I returned to the garden. Richie was there, holding the ball impatiently. Very rarely did I feel that I wanted to tell any of my friends about what I was doing in this other part of my life. The indifference I encountered at Crazy Tots years before had taught me that they were unlikely to be remotely interested. But on this occasion, I *did* feel the need. 'What's up?' Richie said.

'Not much. I just got this part. Should be fun.'

'What is it?'

'Harry Potter. I'm playing the baddie.'

'Harry who?'

'Don't worry about it. Are we finishing this game or what?'

I lost that game, but I won a part.

And so it all began.

8

THE TABLE READ

or

KISS KISS KISS ON THE BUM

The scripts were written. The casting was complete. But day one of filming can't be the first time that cast meets script. The filmmakers need to know that everything's going to work when the camera starts rolling, and that it's all sounding as it should. Which is why you need a table read. The clue's in the name. You all sit down at the table, and you read the script out loud.

I'd been to table reads before, but nowhere near on this scale. It was more than a little daunting when I saw the size of the cast. We rocked up to a vast hangar at Leavesden Studios to find an enormous square of tables, twenty feet by twenty feet, and a crowd of adult actors, child actors and the children's chaperones. We kids all said hello and hung out a bit, but much like my character I thought I was too cool for school. The chaperones were all asked to sit around the edges of the hangar, so while my mum settled down with a nice cup of tea, I took my place at this imposing table. I looked around and took in some of the people that would be part of my life for the next ten years. Daniel, Rupert and Emma I'd met, of course. It seems strange to say it now, but theirs were by no means the most famous faces in that hangar, not that I realised it at the time. Some of the most recognisable British actors of recent years were gathered in that space. Sir Richard Harris was at one end of the table, Dame Maggie Smith at another. Richard Griffiths, John Hurt, Julie Walters ... I was surrounded by acting royalty, but I didn't really know who many of them were. I was nervous, but if I had understood what kind of company I was keeping, I'd have been a hell of a lot *more* nervous.

There were exceptions. Along one side of the table was a serious-looking man with a familiar face and a distinguished nose. It was Alan Rickman and I was terrified, not because of the menace he exuded as Severus Snape, but because I loved the film *Robin Hood: Prince of Thieves* and was obsessed with Alan's performance as the dastardly Sheriff of Nottingham. To be in the same room as the Sheriff himself was enough to penetrate even my veneer of schoolboy cockiness. Along another side of the table was a rather less serious-looking man with a comic sneer that makes me laugh to think about it even now. Rik Mayall was a hero to me and my brothers, especially Ash. We'd grown up watching *The Young Ones* and *Bottom* and Rik Mayall routinely had us on the floor. I couldn't wait to get home and tell him I'd met 'Rik with a silent P'. I might have been surrounded by dames and sirs, but it was Rik that I couldn't believe I was in the room with.

In front of me was my script. I'd flicked through it, concentrating on my part, but hadn't read the whole thing. In later films, the scripts were individually watermarked so if one of them leaked out, they would know whose it was. These were not watermarked, but that's not to understate their importance.

The script was gospel. Jo Rowling was rightly very protective over her stories and Steve Kloves, who adapted the books into screenplays, was on a fairly tight leash. Of course, he couldn't include everything, otherwise the films would have been seven hours long. But once the script was approved, there was very little wiggle room to mess with it. That said, it was important to hear it out loud because only then can you identify bits that don't work, or are too slow or too boring. And although I didn't know it at the time, the table read can be a ruthless procedure for actors involved. If, on hearing it out loud, the filmmakers don't like one person's accent against another's, or something just doesn't sound right, they'll think nothing of cutting or replacing the actor involved. It happened with Rik Mayall, although not at the table read. He played the part of Peeves, the mischievous poltergeist, and filmed all his scenes. You'd think that there couldn't be a more perfect piece of casting, but for some reason or other his part was cut.

We went round the table introducing ourselves. *Hi, I'm David Heyman and I'm one of the producers. Hi, I'm Daniel and I'm playing Harry Potter. I'm Richard and I'm playing Albus Dumbledore. I'm Tom and I'm playing Draco Malfoy.* Robbie Coltrane and Emma Watson were sitting next to each other. When their turn came to introduce themselves they exchanged identities. *I'm Robbie and I'm playing Hermione Granger. I'm Emma and I'm playing Rubeus Hagrid.* I found it hilarious at the time - huge Robbie and tiny Emma swapping parts - and it was typical of Robbie Coltrane to ease any tension in the room with his brilliant sense of humour. He understood that you couldn't have a room full of kids and try to take everything too seriously, and he had a knack of lightening the atmosphere.

Not that I wasn't still nervous. The table read started. Everybody was brilliant. I could sense my first lines coming up, pages and pages in advance. I'd highlighted my dialogue and folded the pages it was on. I repeated the lines over to myself in my head. *It's true then, what they're saying on the train. Harry Potter has come to Hogwarts.* I had a sudden flashback to that moment, years before, when I played Tree Number One, forgot my line and waddled off in tears. Surely that wouldn't happen now ...

My moment came. I hurried through my line and all was fine. Most of my nervousness disappeared. Halfway through, we had a break. Rik Mayall jumped up and shrieked: 'Race you to the toilets!' He sprinted off like a demented Pied Piper, with twenty kids running after him. Me first.

Making a film is a serious business. People have invested a lot of money in the project. They have skin in the game and they want to see that their investment is being properly handled. There were plenty of bigwigs at the table read that day, doing just that. But I had the sense, thanks to people like Robbie and Rik, that filming *Harry Potter and the Philosopher's Stone* would be a lot of fun. Would it be successful? Would there be any more films? That, I didn't know. I didn't even really think about it, to be honest. It was still just another film for me at the time. I didn't expect it to be life-changing.

Far more exciting than the table read itself was the opportunity I had, at the end, to pluck up the courage and introduce myself to Rik Mayall. It was Ash's birthday coming up and Mum had his card in her handbag, which I timidly asked him to sign. Very kindly, he obliged. To my absolute and lasting delight, he scrawled: 'Happy Birthday Ash, Love Rik Mayall, XXX on the bum!' Then he danced off, Peeves-like, to entertain some other kids.

My mum looked at the card, shook her head and frowned. 'I really don't know about that, Tom,' she said. 'I don't think it's appropriate.'

'Relax, Mum,' I told her. 'It's a joke.' I tucked the card away like it was treasure. And it *was* treasure. My brothers weren't remotely impressed by my sideline as an actor, but a kiss on the bum from Rik Mayall was worth its weight in gold.

9

DRACO AND DARWIN

or

HOW MALFOY GOT HIS SNEER

My grandfather is brilliant. His name is Nigel Anstey, and he's a geophysicist by trade. An eminent geophysicist, I might add, with a long list of awards and even an award named after him. When the time came to head off on location to film *Philosopher's Stone*, and I needed a chaperone to accompany me, Grandpa got the gig. Mum couldn't leave her job yet again, so my grandmother Wendy came down to help her with the house, while Grandpa and I hit the road.

With his big grey beard, my grandfather looks like Darwin or, if you prefer, like a wise old wizard, which is why, when Chris Columbus first saw him on the staircase at Leavesden Studios while he was chaperoning me to hair and make-up, he thought he'd make a fantastic Hogwarts professor.

INT. THE STAIRCASE, LEAVESDEN STUDIOS. DAY.

An elderly bearded gentleman escorts a scrappy blond kid to the hair and make-up department. They encounter Chris Columbus, who stops for a moment, blinks twice and inclines his head.

COLUMBUS

(with the enthusiasm of an American film director)

Hey, have you read the book?

GRAMPS

(with the reserve of a British academic)

I have.

COLUMBUS

You'd be a great wizard! Ever thought of acting?

GRAMPS

I have not.

COLUMBUS

Well we'd love to have you at Hogwarts! Would you consider it?

A beat.

GRAMPS

I shall.

It was unheard of for a family member of the cast to have a cameo in the films. My grandfather was the exception. In the first film, look for him at the far right of the professors' table the first time the students enter the Great Hall, or when Professor Quirrell announces that there's a troll in the dungeon, or sitting next to Lee Jordan during the first Quidditch match. He also had an uncanny resemblance to Richard Harris, so was often used as Dumbledore's body double to line up shots. However, his influence over the film extended to more than some brief cameos in front of the camera.

My grandmother enjoys stories about fairies, spirits, magic, ghosts and goblins. I've inherited that passion from her. My grandfather, on the other hand, is an arch-scientist. He's slow, methodical and very rational. My brothers and I used to play chess with him, and he would repeatedly wipe the floor with us, although he insisted on taking the full five minutes between moves. We lost out of boredom half the time. But for all his rationalism, he has a huge passion for the arts. He loves opera, classical and contemporary music, theatre, poetry and film. So he was, I think, pleased to be a part of the film, and pleased to help me prepare for the role.

I had a tendency to stumble when I spoke. My words would run into each other out of sheer enthusiasm and I even started to develop a slight stammer. My grandfather taught me to slow my speech down. To articulate clearly and precisely. It's an important lesson for any young actor, but my grandfather furnished me with more than just generic advice. He was instrumental in developing one of Draco's most distinctive characteristics: his sneer.

Draco would be nothing without his sneer, so he insisted I needed to practise it. We sat down in front of a mirror in a little bed and breakfast on location, trying to get it just so. He told

22 September 1987

Surrey

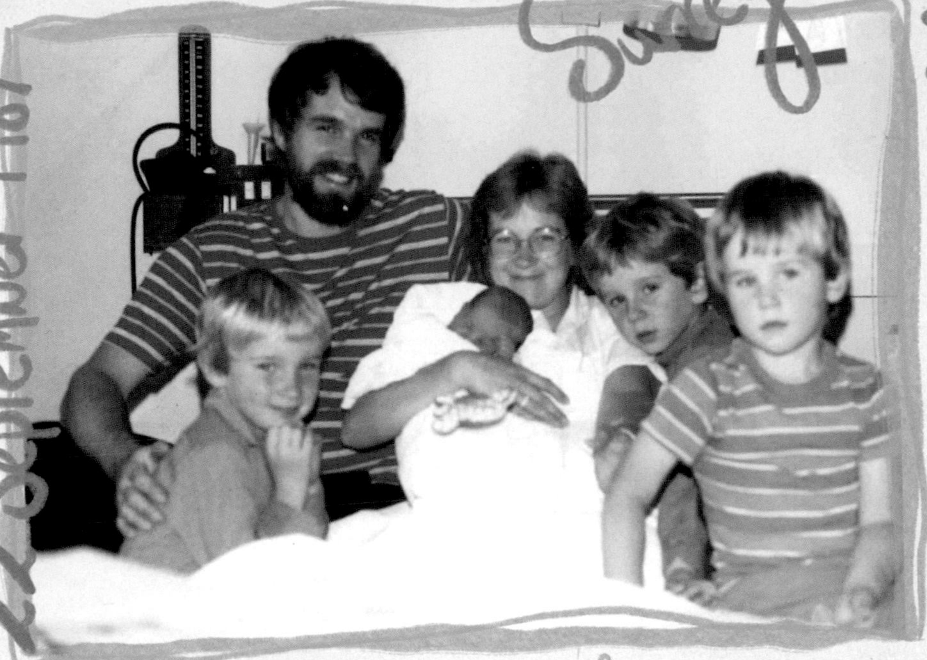

My parents, brothers & me, a few minutes after I was born.

Dad and me on holiday.

Me & Mum

FRANCE 1993

Family camping trip.

THE FELTON BOYS

Jink Chris me Ash

With Jink, Ash & Chris

One of my first acting gigs,
In a nativity play.

In dodgy Gryffindork colours :-

School

...NEW YORK

With my pretend grandfather in my first advert.

My real grandfather, at the High Table in the Great Hall.

abacus agency
39 Horne Road
Shepperton
Middlesex TW17 0DJ
Tel: 01932 568224
Fax: 01932 568225
Full C.V's available from Agency

TOM
FELTON

Television: James in BUGS -Carnival Films
Film: Peagreen in THE BORROWERS -Working Title Films
Radio: Hercule in HERE'S TO EVERYONE. Ioeth in THE WIZARD OF EARTHSEA, -Both BBC

COMMERCIALS

SINGS. VIOLIN

Height 4 feet 6 inches Blue Eyes D.O.B 22 9 87 *Tony Arnold 1996*

Larking about while filming The Borrowers.

Me and mum at Shepperton Studios.

1996

With Jodie Foster in Malaysia filming Anna and the King.

A Slytherin in the making

2001

Early Potter days.

Muggle Studies with Emma and Alfie.

Harry Potter Star Is Carp Crazy!

He's great at Quidditch and loves nothing more than hopping on a broomstick! But carp fishing is more important than any of this to Tom Felton, the lad who plays Draco Malfoy in the Harry Potter films...

Angler Fact File

My happy place as a young teenager.

Chris Columbus directing us in our first big scene.

Thanks Devon. Thanks Ja

First DVD launch by the Hogwarts Express.

irst Name : Thomas Surname : Felton

ate : January 2002 Form: 9 SA

ouse Points Gained	0
ates	9
bsences (out of 148)	77
niform Marks	0

FORM TUTOR'S COMMENT

Thomas is a confident and interesting member of the form who has a good sense of humour. However, as this report shows, many of his teachers are concerned about his progress. This has been hindered by his absences, but the situation worsened by lack of effort and poor behaviour whilst in school. Thomas does not contribute to school life and the form group which is a shame as I feel that he has much to offer.

Signed: S Tiller

HEAD OF YEAR'S COMMENT

Thomas must put more effort into his studies whe is in school, and avoid distracting others. We expect more from Thomas.

Signed:

HEAD'S/DEPUTY HEAD'S SIGNATURE

Signed: D Evans

An early mixed review.

Robbie

Hagrid and the spooky rubber Tom.

Martin

Disney Awards with Emma.

The brothers visit Jink at Uni.

Me and mum on the way to a Potter premiere.

2007

With Chris Columbus in New York.

me to imagine that I was smiling about something terrible. If the smile's too big, it's too happy. So he made sure it was small and slimy. Once we got that, he taught me to lift and flare my nostrils, as if smelling something disgusting. 'Perfect,' he said. 'Now do it with one nostril.' And finally, he encouraged me to channel into my sneer the frustration I felt at being the youngest, smallest, weakest sibling. There was plenty of frustration to work with! Every younger sibling feels hard-done-by, and if Draco could treat the rest of the cast the way I felt my brothers sometimes treated me, I'd surely be doing something right.

I did what he said. I sat in front of the mirror and I remembered all the times my brothers had called me a maggot and a runt. I remembered all the times they'd hogged the remote control and never let me get a look-in. I remembered the time Jink was winding me up while we were playing on the fourth-hand pool table my dad had picked up from Dorking car boot sale. I'd picked up my cue and hurled it at him like a javelin. Very selfishly he ducked, and the javelin flew straight through, and shattered, the glass panels in our back door.

Of course, my brothers will always be my best friends, and my home was nothing like Malfoy Manor, but a happy, fun, loving place. Draco is the product of a dark, abusive family, and I'm a product of a loving one. But those sessions with my grandfather in front of the mirror taught me something important about the craft of acting. An actor brings something of themselves to a part, working with elements of his or her own life and fashioning them into something different. I'm not Draco. Draco's not me. But the dividing line is not black and white. It's painted in shades of grey.

10

UNDESIRABLE NO. 1 (PART 2)

or

GREGORY GOYLE AND THE EXPLODING HOT CHOCOLATE

Making a film is a collaboration. The Harry Potter films were the product of hundreds of brilliantly creative imaginations, from Jo Rowling, through the art departments and camera teams, to some amazing actors. For me, though, the glue that bound them all together for the first two films, the guy who made them what they were, was the director Chris Columbus.

I was a fan of his without even knowing it. He'd made some of my favourite films growing up, including *Mrs Doubtfire* and the *Home Alone* films with Macaulay Culkin, whose own fans I briefly stole as a nipper in New York. But what kid thinks about who the director is when they're watching a film? If I'd been unperturbed about acting alongside Jodie Foster or John Goodman, I was certainly going to be unmoved about working with a director I'd never heard the name of. That soon changed. Columbus quickly became something of a mentor to me on set, and without him my performances would have been unquestionably different.

Columbus had an innate understanding about how to work with children and how to get the best out of us. I guess you don't make a film like *Home Alone* without having somewhat of a playful, childish touch. He understood that if you put twenty kids in a room together, it won't take long before they're all mucking around. (Having thumb wars and playing slapsies were particular favourites.) He made no attempt to stifle that. On the contrary, he encouraged it. He had a brilliant ability to not be consumed by how big the project was. He did that by larking about. One of his larks was setting up a little basketball court, just one net, right in the middle of the studios. To start with it was just for him, so that at lunchtime he could shoot a few hoops. Two or three people joined him, then I asked if I could play. 'Sure dude, come on in, come on in!' Eventually, about eight of us would have our lunch then go and play for 45 minutes. Trouble was, after 15 minutes, my hair and wardrobe would be drenched with sweat and every ounce of my pale make-up would be slopping down my face. Columbus got told off by hair and make-up for letting us kids get into that state. 'Sorry, dude,' he told me, genuinely regretful. 'I want you to play but we just can't.' (I still snuck on a few times after that, but I kept my sweating to a minimum.)

Columbus was not a big advocate of telling us what to do or how to act. He possessed a critical knowledge of what made a shot work from behind his monitor. He then seemed to know exactly what to say to each individual to get what he needed out of us. It was also often more about what he *didn't* say than what he *did* say. His strategy was sometimes to fix the environment so that the performances of his child actors happened naturally and organically. The best example of this is when we first entered the Great Hall. All the kids were purposely kept away from that set until the day we were to film the scene. In the meantime, Columbus made sure that everything was magnificently perfect. The tables were set, the background artists all in place. Hundreds of flaming candles hung from the ceiling on fishing lines (which later melted, causing the candles to plummet). Dumbledore, Hagrid, Snape - and my grandpa - sat at the head table in full regalia. There was no starry sky, of course, just an enormous scaffold for a ceiling, but it was impossible to enter that space for the first time and not be awestruck. The reaction of the Hogwarts first years that you see on screen was genuine. They were as astonished as they looked, just as Columbus cleverly intended. He didn't have to tell us to do anything. He just had to engineer the perfect circumstances for the response he was after. (Of course, I was still outwardly displaying some of my world-weary, meh, nothing-impresses-me attitude, so despite being as impressed as everyone else I may have worn a slightly less enchanted expression. I've no doubt that this was all part of Columbus's plan: my attitude fitted the part perfectly.)

Columbus's enthusiasm was relentless. His constant refrain was: 'Awesome, man, that's *awesome*!' We actually started mimicking him towards the end of the second film with our own takes on 'Awesome, man!', but I'm absolutely certain he wouldn't have minded that. In fact, he would have encouraged it. He wanted us to be cheeky, to be having fun, because he knew that it would translate directly onto the screen.

One-on-one, his directing technique was equally cunning. Because he was such a great guy, the young cast were all keen to impress him and I was no different. He used to make a big deal of how much he loved to hate Draco. Every time I sneered or oozed superiority, he would call 'Cut!', screw up his face and, with a smile, say: 'Ooh, you *bastard*!' Rather than tell me what he wanted, he would respond positively to those parts of my performance that pleased him. In doing so, he would tease the performance out of me, without stress or demands. For me, that is the sign of a great director.

It can't all be shits and giggles, though. Columbus's laid-back attitude was precision engineered to get the best out of his child actors, but we couldn't be *too* laid-back. With scores of kids on the set, that way bedlam lay. So how do you keep a host of high-spirited hooligans under control when the boss is more focused on making sure they're having fun? Somebody needed to play, if not exactly bad cop to Columbus's good cop, then at least *strict* cop. Enter Chris Carreras: the second crucial Chris on the Harry Potter set.

Carreras was the first assistant director. Columbus's right-hand man. That means he runs the set. It was his responsibility to ensure that everything happened smoothly and on time, that everybody knew what they were doing and when they were doing it. No mean feat when you have a sea of excitable kids to keep in line. Carreras was the right man for the job. He's one of the best-established, most-respected first ADs in the industry, and he rightly ran that set like a drill sergeant. Wherever he went, he had a black whistle round his neck, and on day one he gave a speech to us all. Like Dumbledore announcing to the school that the third-floor corridor was out of bounds to those who did not want to die a most painful death, Carreras held up his whistle and laid down the law: 'If I blow this whistle and you don't stop talking, I *will* send you home.'

Carreras was a nice guy, but we were all a little afraid of him. I don't suppose he ever *would* have sent us home, but he had the gravitas and commanded enough respect for us to believe that he *might*. So whenever he blew that bloody whistle, every kid in earshot stopped what they were doing, shut their pie holes and listened.

With maybe the occasional exception.

Josh Herdman - who played Goyle - and I used to get into a fair bit of trouble. I distinctly remember the very first day we shot at King's Cross station. It was one of the few days my dad chaperoned me and I'm happy to report that I wasn't the only Felton to cause trouble that day. He walked on set and was understandably impressed at the sight of all the props, cameras, crowds of background artists and of course the 'Platform 9 ¾' sign, which had been erected for the first time ever and had to be kept under wraps from the outside world. Dad enthusiastically took out his camera to take a photograph of it. This was, of course, strictly forbidden and contrary to set etiquette. An assistant director saw him from behind and shouted that someone was taking pictures. Cue a swarm of people furiously trying to locate the dastardly paparazzo. Dad quickly hid his camera, pointed in another direction and shouted: 'He went that way!' And so he smoothly avoided a substantial telling-off.

I was less lucky. It was freezing cold that day, so they provided a Costa Coffee hot chocolate for all the kids. I guzzled mine down and put my empty cup on the ground. Josh crushed it flat with his heel. He made it look pretty cool. Josh, however, sipped his slowly and had barely drunk any when Carreras's whistle blew. He put the cup on the ground and stood to attention. I was a little less obedient. Not to be outdone, and assuming that Josh's cup was also empty, I jumped as high in the air as I could and landed on it with both flat feet.

It's quite incredible, the mess an exploding hot chocolate can make to every set of Hogwarts robes in a twelve-foot radius. The last thing a filmmaker on a tight schedule wants is a bunch of soggy, dirty teenagers whose costumes require emergency cleaning. Carreras's face dropped. He strode up to us and gave us a look that would have had Snape himself quaking in his boots. A look that said: you little shit! I was properly scared of Carreras in that moment, and genuinely thought my career as Draco might be over before it had really begun. Happily, I detected the slightest of smiles as he reprimanded me. I'd gotten away with it, although we were never allowed hot chocolate on set again. And while I'd like to say that being the focus of Chris Carreras's wrath kept us in line from that moment on, I'm afraid it would not be the truth ...

• • •

From the very first moment I was offered a part in the Harry Potter films, the rules were clear: I wasn't allowed to do *anything* dangerous. Skiing? No chance. Extreme sports? You've got to be joking. It was the Barclaycard advert all over again. The restrictions made sense. Nobody wants to spend millions of pounds shooting half a film, only to find that you have to reshoot a big chunk of it because one of your actors has to spend the next six months in hospital with three broken bones.

Even minor injuries can — and did — cause a problem. When we were shooting the second film, my friend Richie, whose house I'd been at when my mum called to say I'd landed the role of Draco, came round for a sleepover. We slept in the front room, me on the couch, Richie on the floor. At the time, the Felton family were the proud new owners of a cordless telephone and Richie and I had spent the night making prank calls. The lights were out so that Mum wouldn't know we were still awake.

'Chuck us the phone,' I whispered excitedly.

Richie did just that. He chucked it. Hard. You'd think that being part of the Slytherin Quidditch team, I'd be good with my hands, but as I reached out to catch the phone my seeker skills let me down. The phone cracked me solidly on the forehead. *Shit.* We fumbled our way towards the lightswitch and flicked it on. Richie stared at me. 'What?' I said. '*What?* Can you see something?'

'Oh ... my ... God,' Richie breathed.

A bump the size of a golden snitch had immediately appeared on my forehead. Not great under even normal circumstances. Especially not great when you have a big scene to shoot the following morning in the Great Hall.

Mum called the set first thing. 'Er, Tom's had a bit of an accident ...'

'Right,' replied a long-suffering production person. 'How bad is it?'

'Um, it's not *that* noticeable,' she lied. 'Just a tiny bump on the head ...'

But I walked into hair and make-up that morning to a shocked silence. I looked like something out of a Tom and Jerry cartoon. A make-up lady whisked me into the chair and did her very best to cover up my ridiculous wound, but every shot of me in the Great Hall that day had to be taken from my good side, thanks to Richie's dodgy aim and my inept catching.

So the rules were strictly enforced: do nothing dangerous.

But rules are meant to be broken, right?

That was certainly my approach in those early days of Potter. One of our first location shoots took place at Alnwick Castle in Northumberland, where we filmed the broomstick lesson scene with Zoë Wanamaker as Madam Hooch. That one scene took three or four days at least: time enough for me to get into a good deal of trouble with Alfie Enoch, who played Dean Thomas. Alfie was a year older than me, and a smart, funny guy. He had a professional chaperone rather than his parents or a family member, and like me had a penchant for skateboarding. Which was, of course, strictly forbidden. A reckless young actor could do himself a lot of harm on a skateboard. I'd managed, though, to smuggle one into my suitcase. I soon identified one of those perfectly tarmac'd hills that you sometimes find in the middle of nowhere, and persuaded Alfie that it would be a good idea for us to sneak off and try it out.

It wasn't a good idea. As an idea, it had disaster written all over it. But we didn't care about that. We scarpered up the hill and put it through its paces. I think we had the sense not to stand up on the skateboard, but to ride it more like a bobsleigh. It didn't help our cause one little bit when Alfie's chaperone found us wildly speeding down this hill with little thought for our own safety, or for the hassle we might cause the film if we hurt ourselves. She went absolutely nuts, we found ourselves in extreme disgrace and I was swiftly marked out as a bad influence.

I'd like to think of that as poppycock. Truth is, it wasn't. Almost immediately after filming began, life had started to mirror art and I found myself in a little clique with Jamie and Josh - Crabbe and Goyle. Josh and I had already made a name for ourselves as trouble-makers with the crew, thanks to the exploding hot chocolate at King's Cross, but we soon gravitated towards explosions of a different kind.

We were filming in and around Newcastle and staying at the same hotel, which was cool because we got to hang out after filming. We were very excited when Josh revealed he had managed to bring a blank-firing replica pistol with him. This was something that my mum would never in a million years have let me have anything to do with, and rightly so. It looked identical to a normal handgun, although it would only fire a blank round. No bullets, but still not the kind of thing you want in the hands of a trio of mischievous young teenagers. And that, of course, was half the thrill.

We were desperate to fire the gun, but we couldn't think of a good place to do it. Obviously the hotel was out, and even we knew it would be stupid to allow it anywhere near set. In the end, we waited until the witching hour before we sneaked off to the basement level of a nearby multi-storey car park. The level was empty and I suppose our backwards reasoning was that this would be a safe place to fire the thing without scaring anybody and, crucially, without being caught.

We failed to take into account the acoustics.

If you've ever been in one of those car parks, you'll know how they echo. So imagine the noise a gun makes, albeit a blank firer. Josh cocked the weapon. We braced ourselves.

He squeezed the trigger. The noise was earsplitting. It rang out and echoed through the whole car park. If we'd wanted to fire the gun subtly, we'd chosen pretty much the worst place in Newcastle to do it. We stared at each other in horror as the retort of the gunshot refused to fade. It reverberated and lingered like a howler in the Great Hall.

So we ran.

I don't think I've ever sprinted so fast. Sweating and breathless with panic, we tore out of the car park, back to the hotel and shut ourselves in our rooms. I was terrified that someone might have seen us, that we were going to be reported and hauled up in front of the police or, worse, in front of David Heyman, the producer. What would happen then? Surely we'd be sent home. Surely that would be the end of it? Surely even Chris Columbus would have a sense-of-humour failure at our stupid exploits?

I waited, cold dread in my veins, for the knock on the door or, worse, for the parp of Chris Carreras's whistle. Neither came. We'd dodged a bullet - almost literally. And while we were never so stupid again as to try to discharge a blank firer in a public car park, there's a bond that develops between people when they get up to no good and get away with it. Draco, Crabbe and Goyle were a troublesome trio on the page and on the screen. Some people might take the view that the Slytherin trio were worse in real life, at least in those early days. I couldn't possibly comment.

11

A DAY ON SET

or

SEVERUS SNAPE'S SAUSAGE SANDWICH

Perhaps you imagine a day's filming at the Harry Potter studio set to be a day of wizarding glamour or Hollywood star treatment.

Allow me to burst your bubble.

Don't get me wrong: being an actor on a film set certainly beats being at school. But I've found that the reality is different to most people's expectation.

A typical studio day would start with a knock on my front door at six in the morning. It would be Jimmy (we affectionately called him Crack Bean), my driver of nine years, bright and perky and ready to take me to work. Like any teenager, I was the very opposite of bright and perky at that time of day. I would stumble reluctantly out of bed and walk zombie-like, clutching a pillow, to the car - a dark green BMW 7 Series with a long wheel base that I most definitely did not need. Ensconced in the passenger seat, I'd become an instant carcoleptic and snooze through the hour and a half it took to get from home to the studios, where Jimmy would drop me at the iconic Door 5.

Door 5 led to the dressing rooms, the production office and the art department. It was the shabbiest, most run-down block I'd ever seen. Old rickety stairs, sticky checkerboard lino on the floor. More often than not it would be pissing down with rain outside, or the Tupperware grey of the skies would remind you that this was definitely England, not Hollywood. Still bleary-eyed, I would go to find some breakfast in the canteen: hash browns and beans, good British stodge to fill up a hungry teenager. Then I'd stagger up those rickety stairs to the production office to get my 'sides'. These were mini scripts that comprised the day's order of play and the lines I'd need to know. I was the despair of the second assistant directors, whose job it was to produce and distribute the sides, because I was forever losing them.

Next stop: my dressing room. My route would take me through the art department. It was a truly astonishing place, where supremely talented artists sat round a long Gringotts-esque table, fashioning props for the wizarding world out of clay, or building exquisitely precise scale models of various sets. At the end of the art department was the office of David Heyman. Being called there was like being called to see the headmaster, usually to discuss something important. Daniel, Emma and Rupert had their dressing rooms together at the end of one corridor, with a ping-pong table nearby (side note: young Emma Watson was a very adept ping-pong player). My dressing room was on a different corridor. A plaque on the door said 'Draco Malfoy'. It was the done thing for the plaques to give the character's name rather than the actor's. (For the fifth film, Alan Rickman changed the label on his dressing room door to 'The Half-Blood Prince'.) If anyone thought my dressing room would be a cocoon of outrageous comfort and privilege, they would be disabused of that notion once they'd stepped inside. It was a tiny room, painted white, with a metal clothes rail and a plastic chair. My Hogwarts robes - or whatever costume was required for the day - would be hanging on the rail. I'd change into it and make my way to hair and make-up.

Hair and make-up on the Potter films was a massive operation. The artists would have to get through twenty or thirty actors a day, and I'd probably spend an hour in the chair each morning, more if I was getting my roots done, which happened once every nine days. From time to time I'd go through all that and end up not even being used for the day's filming. (Timothy Spall once told me he acts for free - he's only paid to wait.) We had to be there and ready on the off-chance we were needed for a scene, which often we weren't. This could be a bit frustrating, though it was worse for someone like Warwick Davis, who played Professor Flitwick/Griphook. It would take three or four hours to apply his hair and make-up, and another couple of hours to remove it. A long time in the chair to end up not being called on set.

So now I'm in full Draco regalia, my robes are flowing and my bleached hair is just so. Which means it's time to go to school. And the school in question, alas, was not Hogwarts, but another plain white room down another corridor where one of a number of tutors would be waiting for us. There was a legal requirement that all school-aged kids should receive a minimum of three hours of tutoring every day. That requirement was literally observed to the millisecond: our time in tutoring was measured using stopwatches. The moment we picked our pens up, the clock was on. The moment we put them down to go to set, it was off. Even a five-minute stint would go towards our allotted three hours, and the stop-start nature of the process was hardly conducive to effective learning.

Not that I was particularly interested in learning effectively. I hated tutoring. It was nothing to do with the tutors; my mum had recommended Janet, who had tutored me on *Anna and the King*, and she headed up a team of tutors who did their very best with us. I'd be in a class of three, tops, often with Jamie or Josh because we were generally filming in the same scenes, but my attention was always elsewhere. The moment the call came that we were needed for blocking, I was out of there.

There were eight stages at Leavesden, named A to H. Each stage was essentially a huge warehouse, where they would build the sets in astonishing detail. Into one warehouse they imported countless tons of topsoil and planted actual trees to create the Forbidden Forest. Another contained the water tank, which was the largest in the world at the time. As I've already mentioned, the Great Hall was a masterpiece, situated in the final stage, furthest from Door 5. It was a long walk or, if you were lucky, a fun drive in a golf buggy. (I tried skateboarding there on many an occasion, and even tried driving myself once or twice. I was furiously reprimanded each time.) The journey would take us past myriad white tents where technicians and other crew members were hard at work on whatever was needed for that day's filming. As the films progressed, the way would be littered with pieces of scenery from previous films. You'd pass enormous wizard chess pieces from *Philosopher's Stone*, or the sky-blue Ford Anglia, or - most impressively - the huge snake-head statues that lined the entrance to the Chamber of Secrets. The statues were exquisitely made and looked lifelike and weighty. Only when you got up close did you realise they were made of lightweight polystyrene and weighed practically nothing. Other stages were floor to ceiling with props and nicknacks that would have been a Harry Potter fan's dream to explore.

The most impressive set, which came along in the later films, was the Room of Requirement. It was brimful of random wizarding paraphernalia. There were trunks and chests, musical instruments, globes, vials and strange stuffed animals. There were chairs and books piled to the sky, tilting and teetering so they looked like they were about to fall at any minute (in fact they were held in place by steel rods through the middle). The place was stuffed with all manner of curiosities that you'd typically find in an old antique shop, but by the thousand. You could have spent a year wandering round that set and still not have taken it all in. It was very cool.

Blocking is the process of running through a scene so that when the time comes to film it, everybody knows what they have to do, when they have to do it and, most importantly, where they have to stand. The process is important for the director and the actors because it gives them the opportunity to try out their lines, their movements and their facial expressions in a variety of different ways. For me, the direction was usually to stand in the corner and look miserable, or to go to my usual seat in the Great Hall and be myself. The adult actors had more leeway. It was instructive to watch performers of their calibre evolve their scenes throughout the process. While the text was gospel, the interpretation was fluid and the scenes would gradually come alive.

The blocking process was equally important for the camera team because a scene can have many moving parts and they have to work out the various angles they need to capture. We had the luxury of a huge camera team and plenty of time, so this was an involved job. Imagine filming a scene in the Great Hall. There might be a shot of the doors opening, a shot of the ceiling, of Harry, Ron and Hermione at the Gryffindor table, of Hagrid and Dumbledore at the high table. There might be an argument between Harry and Draco, and the geniuses behind the camera will need to work out how to shoot over Harry's shoulder to get Draco's response. They'll place little bean bags on the floor so that everyone remembers their positions. Often the eye-lines are very different to what feels natural, so they'd put bits of tape around the camera lens so you knew where to look.

Once the blocking was done, we'd still be nowhere near ready to film. It could sometimes take two or three hours to light the set, and not only was there a prescribed amount of time that we kids had to be in education, there was a limit to how long we could legally be on set in one go - and yes, somebody was timing that with a stopwatch, too. So we'd be packed off back to tutoring while our places on set were taken by doubles. These doubles were not lookalikes, exactly, but they were chosen to be about the same height and with the same skin tone as the actors. They replicated our movements while the set was being lit, and we would trudge back to the decidedly less exciting prospect of algebra or something similar with Janet and her team of tutors. With a click of the stopwatch we were back at school until they were ready for us on set to do a take.

At lunchtime we would congregate in the canteen, which was always a fun moment. There was no separation of roles. An electrician would be queuing for his lunch next to a witch and a goblin, then a cameraman, a carpenter and Hagrid. As the films progressed, the shooting schedules became busier, especially for Daniel, Emma and Rupert, and we tended to have our food brought to us to save time. There was never a day, however, that Alan Rickman wasn't to be seen in full, flowing Snape robes, holding his tray and queuing up in the canteen for his lunch like everyone else. I was rather intimidated by Alan from day one. It took three or four years for me to manage more than a slightly terrified and squeaky 'Hi Alan!' whenever I saw him. But seeing him wait patiently, in full Snape mode, for his sausage sandwich took the edge off just a little.

A regular feature of a day's filming would be visitors to set. They would generally be children and mostly the visits would be in aid of a children's charity. Alan Rickman requested by far the most visits for charities that he supported. It seemed to me that he had a group in almost every day. And if anyone understood what a child wanted from a trip to the Harry Potter set, it was him. None of our visitors were that interested in meeting Daniel, Rupert, Emma or, for that matter, me. They wanted to meet the characters. They wanted to put on Harry's glasses, to get a high five from Ron or a cuddle from Hermione. And since Daniel, Rupert and Emma were so similar in real life to their idea of the characters, they never disappointed. It was different for us Slytherins. I might have got the role of Draco in part because of the similarities between us, but I liked to think that I was not *so* Draco-esque that I'd be unpleasant to a group of nervous, excited youngsters. So I'd greet them, all smiles, and be as friendly and welcoming as I could be. 'Hi, guys! Are you having fun? What's your favourite set?' And crikey did I get that wrong. Without exception they'd look aghast and confused. Draco being a nice bloke was as anathema to them as Ron being a dickhead. They didn't quite know how to process it. Alan understood this implicitly. He understood that while they might want to meet Alan Rickman, they'd much rather meet Severus Snape. Whenever he was introduced to these young visitors, he gave them the full Snape experience. They'd receive a clip round the ear and a terse, drawn-out instruction to tuck ... your ... shirt ... in! The kids would be wide-eyed and joyfully terrified. It was a lovely thing to watch.

I'd learn, as the years progressed, that some people find it difficult to distinguish between fact and fiction, between fantasy and reality. Sometimes that could be trying. But I wish I'd had Alan's confidence to remain in character during some of those meet and greets at Leavesden Studios. There's no doubt that in doing so, he brightened many a day.

12

FANS

or

HOW (NOT) TO BE A REAL DICK

The Odeon Leicester Square.

I'd attended a premiere here before, of course, when Ash and Jink covered themselves in glory. I mean, vomit. So the first Harry Potter premiere was not entirely unexplored territory for me. My family and I arrived in a couple of black cabs. I emerged in a suit and tie, shirt untucked, top button undone (much to my grandfather's dismay), and despite the crowd's excitement I allowed myself to enjoy the fans and the cameras and the general mayhem. After the film, though, as we were exiting, a little kid ran up to me. I suppose he was the son of one of the studio bigwigs. He couldn't have been much more than five years old and he confronted me with absolute fury in his eyes.

```
EXT. THE ODEON LEICESTER SQUARE. NIGHT.

                        KID
        Hey! Are you Draco?

                        TOM
        Er, yeah.
```

KID

(angrily)

You were a real dick!

TOM

(perplexed)

Huh?

KID

I said, you were a real *dick*!

TOM

Wait … what?

KID

Piss off!

The kid turns his back on Tom *in a gesture of righteous indignation and disappears into the crowd.* Tom *scratches his head, wondering what the hell just happened.*

I didn't get it, why was he giving me such a hard time? What had I done wrong? Was he criticising my acting? It was only when I turned round to see my grandpa smiling that I realised this was a Good Thing. He explained that the boy was *supposed* to hate me. If a five-year-old has that kind of visceral reaction to my performance, it meant I must have done something right. The penny dropped and I realised that the more of a dick I was, the more that kids hated me, the more fun it would be.

What I didn't fully understand at the time was that certain fans had difficulty distinguishing between Tom the actor and Draco the character. Understandable in a five-year-old, but perhaps a little harder to process in someone older. At an early premiere in America, a woman approached me with a steely glare.

EXT. TIMES SQUARE NEW YORK CITY. NIGHT.

STEELY WOMAN

Why are you *such* a dick to Harry?

TOM

(taken somewhat off his guard)

I'm sorry what?

STEELY WOMAN

Can't you just stop being such an *asshole* to him?

Tom *glances sidelong, clearly wondering if he can make a sharp exit. But he can't. He's trapped.*

TOM

Er, you're joking, right?

It's the wrong thing to say. The woman's steely glare becomes steelier. Her eyes narrow. Her lips thin.

STEELY WOMAN

I am *not* joking. You don't have to be so evil to some poor guy who's lost his parents!

Tom *opens his mouth. Then he closes it. When he opens it again, he chooses his words with care.*

TOM

Righty-ho. Okay. Good point. I'll, er, do my best to be kinder in the future.

It's what the woman wants to hear. Brow furrowed, she nods with satisfaction, turns her back on Tom *and stomps away.*

In a way, the tendency some people have to conflate the character and the actor is a compliment. I don't want in any way to overstate my contribution to the world of Harry Potter and the effect the phenomenon has had on people's lives. If I hadn't turned up to audition that day, somebody else would have had the part, they'd have done it well and the whole project would have been largely the same. But there's some gratification in knowing that my performance crystallised people's notion of the character, even if it meant they occasionally mistook fantasy for reality.

I learned that sometimes it was important not to spoil the magic. Over the years I would find myself being invited to a number of Comic Con conventions, where fans congregate to celebrate their enthusiasm for all manner of films, books and any kind of pop culture. At one of the very first, when I was sixteen, I was sitting in front of an audience of several thousand people, answering questions about Potter. There was a queue in the middle of the auditorium of people waiting to reach a microphone and ask me a question. The turn came for a little girl who was dressed head to toe as Hermione and whose mum held the mic as she was not tall enough. Wide-eyed, she asked: 'What's it like to fly on a broomstick?'

I immediately told her the truth. 'It's incredibly uncomfortable,' I said. 'Basically, they strap you to a bike saddle on a metal pole, and I'm probably never going to have kids as a result.' My answer raised a bit of a laugh, but I could see the magic draining from the little girl's eyes and I instantly knew I'd said exactly the wrong thing. The next day, the same question came up from another little Hermione. 'What's it like to fly on a broomstick?'

I'd learned my lesson. I leaned forward, conspiratorially, winked at her and said: 'Are you eleven yet?'

'No.'

'So you haven't had your letter?'

'No.'

'Just you wait,' I told her. '*Just* you wait.' The girl's face shone and you could sense a real excitement in the audience.

Now, whenever anybody asks me that question (and believe me, they still do), that's the answer I give.

After the release of the first film, I started to receive fan mail via the studio. These days, fans interact on social media, but back then physical letters were a thing. Almost immediately, I started to receive sack loads of them. My fan mail was nothing like as abundant as Daniel, Emma and Rupert's, of course. I believe they had a dedicated team at Warner Brothers just to process their mail. But there was a lot of it. My mum would vet the letters first, to make sure there wasn't anything offensive or obscene, and then I'd spend time reading them all. Make no mistake: as the youngest of four brothers there was absolutely no question of me allowing the receipt of fan mail to go to my head. (Chris: 'Who the fuck would write to him?') Nobody at home gave any indication that they thought it was amazing or even unusual to receive sacks of mail as I did. I'm grateful for that, because reading hundreds of admiring letters could turn a certain type of person in a certain type of environment into a certain type of idiot. I did spend a lot of time reading them, though, at least at first. I felt that since people had given up their time to write to me, it wouldn't be cool to ignore them. I responded to as many as I could. Eventually, however, it became too much. The sheer volume of letters was overwhelming. My mum looked into the possibility of paying someone to manage the fan mail, but it just didn't add up. And so my ability to keep on top of the mail diminished as Draco's profile increased.

Most of the letters I did read were sweet. Some were culturally alien to me. Japanese fans, for example, occasionally sent silver spoons as a good luck charm. So if you ever need a spoon, I'm your man. Sweets and chocolate arrived from every country under the sun, none of which my mum would let me eat in case it was poisoned. One particularly weird piece of fan mail does stick in my mind, however. A chap in America had legally changed his name to Lucius Malfoy, and the name of his house to Malfoy Manor. He wanted me to change my name to Draco Malfoy and go to live with him. My mum kindly declined the offer on my behalf. (Chris: 'Nah, send him away!') It seemed funny at the time. We certainly all had a bit of a laugh about it at home. Only in hindsight do I realise that it could have been just a *tad* sinister.

That was one of many bizarre incidents to come. A Spanish family - two parents, two kids - turned up at my Muggle school one day. They just walked straight in and started looking for me. They were, of course, swiftly escorted out, and I was warned to be careful when I left school. Who knows what that family had in mind or thought was going to happen, but I certainly cycled home a bit faster that day.

I had to normalise this unusual way of growing up, otherwise it would drive me crazy. In some ways I didn't find that too hard. My natural British reserve means that, even now, I'm slightly taken aback when somebody approaches me and says, 'Are you Tom Felton?' I find myself wondering what that's all about. How did that happen? Of course, I always had my three brothers to remind me that I was a maggot. Plus, I understood what it was like to be a fan. There were people I admired, and I saw it in others close to me. I once took part in a Comic Relief sketch with Rupert. It featured lots of well-known faces

- James Corden, Keira Knightley, Rio Ferdinand and George Michael, to name a few - but the star of the show was Sir Paul McCartney. Mum was a massive fan, so I asked Sir Paul if I could introduce her. He graciously said yes, so I went to find my mum and told her, 'Now's your chance!' I took her to say hello, but at the last moment she became too star-struck and couldn't go through with it. Sir Paul came looking for her, but I had to let him down lightly. 'Sorry, mate, you'll have to wait another day to meet her.'

As the years passed, though, and the popularity of the films increased, the world of fandom became harder in some ways. Don't get me wrong, there is something strangely exciting about being recognised, when you realise that a chance encounter with a stranger is a huge event for them. Equally, though, it can be weirdly alienating, especially if you're with other people who aren't a part of that world. A moment sticks in my mind when I was about seventeen years old at Heathrow Airport, and about to fly out to America with my girlfriend at the time. While we were waiting for our flight, we slipped into a shop to buy some snacks and a minute later I felt the familiar prickle that told me I was being watched. I turned to see a group of nineteen (we counted them) foreign schoolgirls staring at me. They all had their hands over their faces and were incredibly giggly. I immediately felt myself squirming and tried to avoid eye contact by picking up a knitting magazine that was close to hand. It was very obvious that they had recognised me, and even more obvious that I wasn't studying crochet patterns, but this was the first time I recall well-meaning fans making me feel uncomfortable. It wasn't just that being surrounded by a crowd of people who want to touch part of your clothing can be a discombobulating experience. There were thousands of people in the airport. The chain reaction of one person recognising me, then two, then four could soon get out of hand. Fortunately for the schoolgirls my mum wasn't there - she can be quite bolshie when people crowd me. I took the photo with them, the fans dissipated and I was left with a curious mixture of embarrassment, relief and gratification. I was starting to learn that fame is a strange drug.

Other fans were, and are, more relentlessly persistent. In a weird way they become part of your life. You develop a relationship of sorts with them, and I found it worthwhile to try to understand why I and other members of the cast became such a focus for them. One British lady seemed - and still seems - to pop up magically wherever I go. I first noticed her when she asked for an autograph during a press tour in Paris, and from that day on she seemed to be everywhere. I'd say yes to an event half an hour before it was due to happen and somehow she'd be there. How she knew to expect me, I have no idea. In the early days, I thought it was pretty unhealthy. It certainly led to my mum becoming furiously protective about me if there was any chance that she would be there. Then, one day, she stood outside an event for four hours simply so that she could give me a card telling me how sorry she was that my dog Timber had passed away. It was a kind, heartfelt gesture and it caused me to re-evaluate my opinion of her. I eventually visited her home and learned that she had never had any children of her own and in her head she had kind of adopted the Potter kids. Since I was the only one who engaged with her in any way, she latched on to me. It was an unusual situation, but a reminder of the importance these stories and films have had in people's lives.

As the actor who played Draco Malfoy, I see myself as a placeholder in people's memories. Seeing me transports them to a different time and place, in the same way that listening to a particular song can be evocative of something else. I've met with fans who have explained that the books and films have helped them through hard times. It's a humbling truth to hear. Jo Rowling once said that her most gratifying moments come when she learns that her work has helped somebody get through a difficult moment in their life, and I agree. Sure, from time to time seeing me causes people to react in unusual ways, but I try to remember that those reactions are a function of the place these stories and films have in people's hearts, and to act accordingly. Just because Draco acts like a real dick, it doesn't mean I have to.

• • •

But it can be difficult.

I'm twenty-five years old, and it's my first time surfing with some friends on Topanga Beach in California. My expert mates are telling me how to do it: what waves to look for, how to get up on to the board, all the technical stuff. I'm not really listening. I'm thinking, *I'm just going to wait until I feel the surfboard move, then I'm going to get up and give it a crack.* The first wave comes. It's a reasonable size. I stand up on the board, maintain my balance and glide all the way in. This surfing business is easy!

Or maybe it isn't. For the next five waves I get completely tumble-dried. I swallow a good pint of seawater, having discovered that being spun round under the water with no sense of which way is up or down can be disorientating and rather scary. Bashed up, I crawl my way out of the ocean on to the sand, yak up the sea water I've swallowed, and wave away my concerned mates. Just give me a minute, okay?

And then I see them. Two young women, standing about twenty metres away, holding a camera, pointing at me and whispering to each other. Not now, I think. Please not now! But they approach, a little bit timidly, and I can tell they're about to say something. I know what they want and I have a massive sense-of-humour failure. I stand up and wave my arms in the air. 'Okay!' I shout. 'Let's do this! Who wants to be in the picture?'

The young women look at each other. A slightly strange look. But sure enough one of them holds up the camera. 'Come on then,' I say. 'I know the drill.'

They look strangely at each other again, then at me. Then, in faltering English with an Italian accent, one of them says, 'With the surfboard?'

'Sure! Whatever! You can have a photo with me and my board!'

They shake their heads. They diffidently hand me the camera. And only then do I realise that they don't have the foggiest idea who I am: they just want me to take their photo with the surfboard as a memento of their trip to California.

I got too big for my boots that day, for sure. I also learned two important lessons. One: assumptions are the mother of all fudge-ups. And two: surfing is really fudging hard.

13

HOW TO FLY A BROOMSTICK

or

THE WASPS AND THE WIMP

What's it like to fly a broomstick? Well, if you've read this far, you'll know that's a loaded question. You'll know that I learned early on not to ruin the magic for the children at Comic Con. And if you prefer to remember Harry and Draco's Quidditch matches as the magical battles that appeared on screen, may I gently suggest you move on to the next chapter.

One of our earliest location shoots was at Alnwick Castle, where I managed to get myself and Alfie Enoch into a sticky slalom skateboarding situation. This was also our first shoot with broomsticks. Zoë Wanamaker was Madam Hooch and the Hogwarts first years were receiving their first flying lesson.

It was not only Madam Hooch and the first years who were in attendance. It was a warm, sunny day and, attracted by the smell of thickly applied make-up and hair gel, swarms of wasps were taking an interest in us. More specifically, they were taking an interest in me. Draco's hairdo required the application of an entire tub of gel each day. My blond locks were so rigid, I might as well have been wearing a Kevlar helmet. And as far as the wasps were concerned, the hair gel might as well have been strawberry jam. They were all over it. Full disclosure: when it comes to wasps, I'm a wimp. While Draco might have been acting too cool for school during the scene, off camera I was flapping around like a landed fish, running from the wasps, squealing and trying to swat them away. (And it's not impossible, of course, that the more people laughed at my ridiculousness, the more I might have played up my apparent distress.)

Madam Hooch to the rescue. Her spiky hair required a similar quantity of gook, so Zoë Wanamaker had the same problem. She gave me a strategy to deal with it. 'Just repeat the words "green trees",' she said.

Huh?

She explained that the wasps weren't going to hurt me and I needed a way to relax around them. Repeating her 'green trees' mantra was a way of doing that. So when you watch Draco in that scene, you can imagine me silently chanting those words in the back of my head, and doing my best not to shriek with terror as wasps circled my rock-hard hairdo.

With the wasps dealt with, the students stood in two lines opposite each other, their brooms on the ground. On Madam Hooch's word, they gave the instruction 'Up!' and, with varying degrees of success, caused the broomsticks to jump into their hands. The approach was that if a piece of magic or any kind of special effect could be achieved practically, that was the best way to do it. This was especially true in the early days, when the visual effects teams had less-advanced technology at their disposal. So what you don't see, when the camera points down the middle of the two lines of students, is the guys lying on the ground behind each broom with a see-saw-like contraption, raising the brooms off the ground and even making them waft around a little bit.

Actually flying the things took a bit more ingenuity. Blokes with see-saws weren't going to cut it. The flying scenes were all done in a studio. Imagine a massive room wrapped in blue canvas - or green in the later years. The broomstick was a metal pole fitted with a deeply uncomfortable bike saddle. There were stirrups for your feet and a harness to stop you falling. They strapped you to the pole so you couldn't fall and they had a more elaborate see-saw device to move you up and down, left and right. They blew fans in your face to make it look as if you had the wind in your hair. And because the background was going to be added digitally, and all your nifty broomstick moves were to be cut in at a later date, it was important that all the players were looking in the right direction for the shot. In order to ensure your eye line was as it should be, a guy held up a tennis ball on a long pole with a little bit of orange tape on it. When the first assistant director shouted 'Dragon!' or 'Bludger!' you had to look at the tennis ball like it was, well, a dragon or a bludger. Sometimes there would be more than one tennis ball up there, and as one looked very much like another, after a while they gave us more individual objects to stare at. We chose pictures of something or somebody close to our hearts. Daniel Radcliffe had a picture of a particularly beautiful Cameron Diaz. I chose a picture of an even more beautiful carp. I mean, there's no competition ...

Shooting a Quidditch match or another big broomstick scene was a slow, painstaking, bum-numbing process. The geniuses behind the camera had to work to an unbelievable level of precision. They would shoot the backgrounds first for reference, then the actors on the broomsticks, so one could be superimposed on the other. The camera movements for both shots had to be precisely the same and there always seemed to be a lot of people manning the cameras and the computers needed to make that happen. Quite what they were doing, I don't know - I was just the guy on the metal pole with the fans blowing in my face, staring at a picture of a stunning carp - but I do know that it seemed to take forever to complete even the smallest amount of footage. We would finish those shooting days distinctly saddle-sore.

• • •

As kids, we desperately wanted to do as much of the stunt work as we could. I still had happy memories of the stunt work I did on *The Borrowers*, and amazingly my little disagreement with the gymnastic beam was yet to dampen my enthusiasm for such activities. Certainly we did a lot more of the stunt work than I imagine they would let us do now. In the scene in *Chamber of Secrets* where Harry and Draco have a duelling competition standing on the table in the Great Hall, we had to create shots where Harry and Draco hit each other with spells, one of which shot me in the air and spun me round. That was all achieved practically. I wore a full body harness with a wire coming out of the back, which they wrapped around me several times. Give the wire a good tug and Draco's going to spin. I remember thinking at the time that this was pretty cool. There were maybe a hundred background artists there, and I was up on the table doing my heroic stunt work. Never mind that it was a painful business, or that it left me with a nasty bruise where the cable rubbed into me. This was a fun moment for a slightly cocky teenage actor. Stunt work is cool, right?

Well, yes and no.

The vast bulk of the stunt work was done not by us but by the stunt team. I have nothing but respect for those men and women who push themselves to extremes in the name of film-making, simply so that an audience can be entertained. Pretty much every time you see somebody falling from a broom, or jumping, or being bashed about, you can be almost certain it's one of the stunt team rather than us. I might have felt like the big guy during the duelling scene, but in fact the stunt artists took the brunt of that by far. They seemed to spend a lot of time - especially during *Chamber of Secrets* - working with a piece of equipment called a Russian swing. Imagine an ordinary playground swing but larger and with metal bars instead of ropes. The stunt performer stands on the platform and it swings back and forth, back and forth until its arc is as long as can be. Then, at the peak of the arc, the performer jumps high into the air and falls onto a crash mat. It looked fun, but it was definitely a job for the pros. And the pro that I had the most involvement with was the incredible David Holmes - or Holmesey to us.

Holmesey was Daniel's stunt double from the beginning and also mine from the second film onwards. Given the various escapades of Harry and Draco, it meant he was kept busy. He routinely used to do stunts dressed as Harry in the morning, go off for lunch and come back to do stunts dressed as Draco in the afternoon. He was an Olympic-standard gymnast from a very early age, and in any shot where you see Daniel or me apparently doing something dangerous, you can be fairly sure it was actually Holmesey. And during the filming of *Deathly Hallows* it was brought home to us all that stunt work is not an activity to be approached naively.

Stunt artists do everything they can to minimise the risk of their job. But they can't eliminate it completely - there's no totally safe way of falling from a great height, or being hit by a car - and it is impossible to legislate for an unexpected turn of events. Which is exactly what happened when we were filming *Deathly Hallows*. Holmesey and the rest of the team were rehearsing with a stunt that involved him flying through the air and hitting a wall, wearing a harness and suspended by a high-strength wire. Something went wrong. The wire yanked him back and Holmesey hit the wall far harder than he should have, before falling to a crash mat below. He knew immediately that something was wrong. Paramedics rushed him to hospital, where he learned that he was paralysed from the waist down, with very limited use of his arms, and would be that way for the rest of his life.

Naturally, everyone involved in making the films was distraught. Imagine going from being able to do a backflip on the spot, to lying in a hospital bed being told you'll never walk again. Sure, it's a risk that stunt performers take every day at work but the reality, when it happens, must be earth-shattering. A lesser man than Holmesey might let it faze him and obviously he now lives a very difficult life. But he is the bravest, most strong-willed person I've ever had the pleasure of knowing. He has the heart of a lion and remains one of my closest, dearest friends. When he was in hospital, the studio brought him food, much to the envy of the other patients on his ward. So Holmesey insisted that the studio should cook for everyone on the ward - either everyone should have it or no one should. That was Holmesey through and through. Despite his challenges, he continues to bring us so much joy, and his determination to live as normal and active a life as possible is a true inspiration. He tirelessly raises money for the hospital that saved his life, and has his own production company. He is a constant reminder to me that stunt artists on film sets deserve a great deal more credit than they receive. The actors might get all the adulation, but so often it's the stunt artists that make us look good and Holmesey is the best of them. He's a beacon of light.

In Holmesey's honour, we now have an annual Slytherin vs Gryffindor cricket match to raise money for the Royal National Orthopaedic Hospital, where he was treated in the days following the incident. Radcliffe and I are team captains, and the old Hogwarts grudges have by no means been diminished by the years. I really don't have to tell you which house is in the lead, do I?

14

THE BEST OF BOTH WORLDS

or

BROOMSTICK PRICK

It was not cool to be Draco.

As soon as Daniel, Emma and Rupert were cast, their lives changed. They left school and from that point onwards Potter was their life. They were in a bubble, for better or worse, and all chance they had of a normal childhood was practically gone. It wasn't like that for me. I was one week on, one week off, whereas they were constant. Outside of Potter I went to a normal school, had normal friends and tried very hard to be a normal teenager.

Perhaps you know some normal teenagers. Perhaps you *are* a normal teenager. If so, you'll know that being marked out as odd is not a good thing. So yeah, with my bleached hair and my regular absences from the classroom, it was not cool to be Draco. To plenty of people in the school corridors I was the Harry Potter Wanker. I was the Broomstick Prick.

And so, perhaps I overcompensated a little. I acted up. My prepubescent cheekiness developed into something more disruptive. Remember that I'd moved from an exclusive school where academia was the be-all and end-all, to a normal school where your coolness rating depended upon your ability to source cigarettes, or your prowess on the skateboard or BMX.

I started smoking, and I've already told you about my escapade in HMV. I wasn't the naughtiest kid in the school, not by a long way, but I did feel the need to offset my other life with a bit of normality. I was routinely late for school, and forever bunking off PE or disappearing on my bike to get some sweets. Often I got away with it. My schedule was changeable - I was often out of lessons because I was filming - so the teachers would assume that I was off doing something legitimate. When I was in class, I was far from the model student. I don't think I was *terrible*, but I was forever doodling on my books, chatting with friends or winding up the teachers. I used to keep a MiniDisc player in my pocket, with the headphone wire running along my sleeve to my wrist. It meant I could sit in class, resting my cheek on my palm, listening to music. I thought it was a genius move. My teachers took a different view. I lost count of the times an exasperated teacher said, 'You have to have the last word, Felton.' And because I *did* always have to have the last word, I'd reply, 'Absolutely, sir!' with what I hoped was a winning grin.

The trouble is, the older you get, the less disarming your cheekiness becomes. I can see now that to disappear filming for weeks at a time before rocking up at school with a bit of an attitude almost certainly would have come across as arrogant to the teachers. They afforded me no special treatment. Quite the opposite. I remember one teacher putting me in my place by mocking my hair colour and asking me who'd cracked an egg on my head after I'd once again insisted on having the last word. Even in drama lessons, where you might imagine I would have thrived, I was disruptive. I had no problem going onto a major film set and pretending to be a wizard flying a broomstick with a fan in my face, watching some bloke waving around a tennis ball on a pole. That took place in a safe environment, surrounded by like-minded people, and it wasn't going to affect my social standing one bit. But to act in a drama class in front of lots of other teenagers who'll laugh at you if you get it wrong and even if you get it right? That was a completely different kettle of fish. My defences went straight up. No doubt it outwardly looked like regular teenage disdain. I'm sure my teachers thought I was giving them the full Draco, but it was more complicated than that. I flunked drama with a series of Ds (although that didn't stop one drama teacher asking me, tongue in cheek, if I could get him a part in the films).

So I failed to earn the enduring respect of my teachers during my time at school, with perhaps one exception. Every school child needs a Dumbledore in their life. For me it was Mr Payne, the headmaster. I'd missed a few weeks at the beginning of his first term at the school, and so I hadn't met him until one day when he knocked on the door of my music class, where my mate Stevie and I were sat at a keyboard making up our own songs. He asked to see me. I followed him outside, unsure why I'd been called out by the headmaster. It was nothing sinister. 'You've not been here for the last few weeks,' he said. 'My name's Mr Payne, I'm going to be your head teacher for the rest of your time here, and I wanted to introduce myself.'

I immediately thrust out my hand and said: 'Tom Felton, nice to meet you.'

It was plainly not the response he was expecting. It was the response of a kid used to spending a lot of his time in the company of adults, someone with one foot in a different world. The response of a kid trying to disarm him. He could easily have dismissed that gesture, or found it thoroughly inappropriate. But he didn't. After a moment's hesitation he shook my hand and smiled.

And he carried on smiling, even when I found myself up in front of him for some misdemeanour, as I regularly did. He was always fair, never sarcastic. He was endlessly patient and excited to share his love of his subject, maths. Unlike lots of other teachers, he treated me like a young adult. Perhaps he understood that my behaviour came not from a desire to make anybody else's life difficult, but from an unconscious need to impose some normality into my existence. Maybe he was just a nice guy. All I know is that he had an anchoring effect on my life back then. I've often thought that I'd like to go back and repeat that handshake as an adult. If you're reading this, Mr Payne, thank you.

• • •

Normality was the goal. It wasn't always achievable.

Some friends and I used to go fishing at a couple of ponds in Spring Grove at the bottom of my street. Those ponds didn't hold much in the way of fish, but that wasn't really the point. It was a place to hang out, smoke secret cigarettes and, if we were lucky, land the occasional carp. I used to tell my mum I was sleeping over at a friend's house, he'd do the same, and we'd actually spend all night by the water's edge with our rods, our cigarettes and a disgusting tin of cold Spam for sustenance. Living the dream.

One evening I was there with three mates. Our rods were out and we'd set up for the night, just as we had any number of times before. We were chatting easily, having a bit of a laugh together, when I suddenly heard voices in the distance, but getting nearer. Minutes later, a crowd of about forty kids came into view. I felt a shard of ice in my stomach. I didn't know these kids - they were perhaps a couple of years older than me - but I was sufficiently streetwise to interpret their intentions. It was a mob of bored youths from the area, amusing themselves by marauding the streets and causing trouble. I knew instinctively, as they approached, that they would think they'd hit the jackpot if they twigged that they'd come across the Broomstick Prick. If that happened, I was in proper trouble. Everything about their demeanour told me they were up for a fight. And with forty of them against four of us, I didn't like the odds.

I kept my head down and tried to disappear behind my friends. I figured that, in a situation like this, they wouldn't want to be associated with the Harry Potter Wanker and would do what they could to keep me out of the mob's line of sight.

I was half right. They certainly didn't want to be associated with me.

Before I knew what was happening, my three mates scarpered. I couldn't believe it. A few of the boys picked up my fishing rods and threw them into the lake, by which time the rest of them had worked out who I was. I wanted to run, but my feet were planted to the ground in fear. A couple of boys sidled up to me and started to push me about a bit. They both had lit cigarettes in their hands and they poked the burning ends into my face, much to the crew's amusement. It sounds dramatic - it *was* dramatic - but far worse was the suppressed threat of violence that seemed to hum around the mob. Even if I found the strength to run, they'd be all over me, grabbing clumps of my bleached hair and grinding my face into the dirt.

The wider group moved ever closer to me. I tried to step back. They kept advancing as I slipped and staggered in the mud, and prepared myself for what was to come.

And then, from somewhere behind me, I heard the screech of a car braking hard. I glanced anxiously over my shoulder and saw the tiny Peugeot owned by my brother Chris. I hadn't called him. He didn't know where I was or that I was in trouble. He'd turned up completely by chance and I've never been more pleased to see anyone in my life. He climbed out of the car and found himself immediately surrounded by a few of the crew. Chris is quite a presence, with his shaved head and his earrings, and his arrival had an immediate impact on the gang. They sheepishly lost interest in giving me a hard time, allowing me to stagger further back and put some distance between us. Chris approached. Words were exchanged. I couldn't hear what he said in his quiet voice. To this day I don't know. All I do know is that a minute later the gang had buggered off.

Who knows? Maybe I'd have attracted that kind of aggro even if I wasn't the Wizarding Wanker. But there's no doubt that my bleached hair and claim to fame made me more of a target. If Chris hadn't turned up at just the right moment, it could have ended very differently.

I learned, from that incident and others, to be careful. My life was good, but it was also occasionally scary. When I was fifteen someone stole my bike - my prized possession Kona Deluxe - from the school bike shed. Whoever took it left a note saying: 'We know where you live, we've got our eyes on you and we're going to kill you.' I don't suppose whoever wrote that really meant it. More likely it was just a misplaced attempt at bravado. But it was a terrifying message to receive and for some time I was petrified that I would run into a nutter who would carry out the threat.

I developed a kind of Spidey-sense, an inbuilt radar that told me I was about to be recognised and a situation had the potential to kick off. I remember standing in line to get into an under-18 nightclub in Guildford that my friends had coaxed me to come along to, head down, eyes to the floor, because I knew it would only take one person to say 'Hey, are you ...' and the dominos would start to fall and my evening would take a distinct turn for the worse. Half of me thought it would be fine - the people queueing up outside that club were definitely not the types to be into Harry Potter, if you get my drift. But even so, as the line became a little rowdier and the elbowing a little more frequent, the Spidey-sense kicked in and I knew I had to get out of there. I'd learned from past experience that this was not a good environment for me. I decided that I could forego an evening in the nightclub for a quiet life. Collar up, head down, without explanation, I left for home.

• • •

As I said, it was *not* cool to be Draco.

But here's the thing. Looking back at my Muggle life, the good experiences outweighed the bad. I am pleased to have spent at least some of my time in that normal school with normal people having - by and large - a normal experience. I'm pleased to have had the sarcastic teachers and the classmates who couldn't give two hoots about my other life. Part of me is even pleased about the cigarette butts in the face. They were all part of the regular rough and tumble of a normal childhood. At the very least, they were not part of the cloistered upbringing I could easily have had forced upon me. I'd have been a very different person if I hadn't been given the opportunity to experience the ups and downs of a normal life alongside the madness of being part of Harry Potter. As it was, I had the best of both worlds.

15

TRANSFIGURATION TROUBLES

or

MAGGIE AND THE MILLIPEDE

Filming the Harry Potter films required the use of live animals. Owls, rats, dogs, snakes, you name it. There was a special holding area at Leavesden Studios where the animals were kept. I'm a dog lover, so I fondly remember the half dozen or so dogs that were there to play Fang, Hagrid's pet. They were huge, lumbering animals half the size of a horse, and you couldn't get too close: one shake of those enormous jowls and you'd be covered in a thick layer of doggie slobber. In any case, the animals weren't there to be petted and prodded and poked. On screen you might see Harry quietly holding an owl, but behind the camera there's likely to be a hundred people, with lights and sound effects. It's not easy to get an animal to do what you want it to do with all that commotion going on.

So there was a method. The trainers brought the animals on to the set hours before the children, the rest of the cast or even the crew were invited on. They rehearsed what they were supposed to do tirelessly: the owl that drops off a letter (or a howler) would have been practising for hours before the set became live. No matter how well rehearsed it is, however, when the animals do come on to a live set, and there are hundreds of kids talking, lights flashing, smoke machines, fire effects and all sorts of other distractions, they are very likely to be distracted. So we were taught very early on that when animals are around, you *must* be calm around them.

Over the years, as the films became bigger, so did the animal holding area. By the end there were hundreds of fantastic beasts at Leavesden, and everyone enjoyed working with them. But you know what they say about working with children and animals. I don't doubt that Dame Maggie Smith found herself reflecting on that old maxim while we were filming *Chamber of Secrets.*

Dame Maggie has a commanding presence. I was lucky enough to get to know her just as Maggie before I really understood what a legend she is. Like Professor McGonagall herself, Maggie exudes a quiet, calm authority, and she's always hiding a wry smile. And like Alan Rickman she has the ability to be really quite stern while also remaining incredibly patient. It's a useful quality when you have a film set full of misbehaving kids who have no real idea who you are, no concept of the esteem in which you're held. And I'm sorry to say that I tested that patience somewhat more than I should have in the early days.

The scene was Professor McGonagall's Transfiguration lesson. The students were sitting at old-fashioned sloping school desks, the kind with the lid that opens up, and all around the room were cages with animals in them. Think snakes, monkeys, toucans and even a rather ill-mannered baboon. The baboon in question was - how can one put this? - unaware of the niceties of social interaction and set etiquette, and in particular he was unaware of what behaviour it is appropriate to exhibit in front of a bunch of kids. Which is my roundabout way of saying that we had to cope with the distracting intrusion of a self-pleasuring primate during the filming of the scene. There was many a take that had to be discarded because of a wanking baboon in the background. They had to move the poor creature several times to stop his vigorous pastime ruining the shot, and you can imagine the chaos that ensued each time one of us kids saw what was happening out of the corner of our eye and shouted, 'Oh my God, look at the baboon!'

For the scene, each child was individually given an animal. Mine was a gecko on a little branch. The animal guys had tied a length of fishing twine to its body to stop it scurrying away, and I was told in no uncertain terms not to grab it by its tail. Apparently a gecko's super power is that it can shed its tail and grow a new one, so if you hold it there's a good chance the tail will come off in your hand. He was a fairly docile little chap. He sat on his branch, good as gold, and I just about resisted the urge to test out his super power. Like the gecko, most of the animals distributed around the class were perfectly chilled. (More chilled than the baboon, at least.) There was a mellow shrew and some pretty decent-sized but well-behaved insects.

And then there was Josh Herdman's millipede.

The millipede was easily as thick as my thumb and as long as my forearm. It had a billion legs and seemed to be incapable of not moving. It wriggled and squirmed around the sloping desk next to me, the polar opposite of my immobile gecko. It was fascinating to watch, and irresistible to poke.

Any ordinary school kid would have used a pencil for that purpose, but we had better tools to hand. We had wands! In the spirit of scientific inquiry, we (gently) poked and prodded that poor millipede, and we learned something astonishing. Poke it enough, and it will roll up, hedgehog-like, into a little Cumberland sausage shape. And when that happened, it would slide

slowly

down

the

sloped

desk.

The hilarity this sliding millipede caused me and Josh was off the scale. With each poke, sausage and slide we'd completely corpse.

Normally, when somebody corpsed on set, it was funny. Chris Columbus had almost infinite patience, and you can hardly take pains to create a fun filming environment and then give people grief for having a laugh. But it can't be constant hilarity. There comes a point where you have to get some footage in the can. And so Columbus came up with a system to deal with eventualities such as this. Any time one of us disturbed a take, we were given a red card. A red card meant you had to put ten pounds into a bag and at the end of the shoot, all the money was donated to charity. It was a good plan to keep us on the straight and narrow, but it didn't always work. Rupert Grint was one of the worst offenders. I believe he put in over £2,500 during the first two films alone, such was his inability to control himself when the giggles hit. It certainly didn't work on this occasion. Each time the call of 'Action!' rang out, Josh or I would poke the millipede in an attempt to keep it on its mark. Yet again it would slide

slowly

down

the

sloped

desk.

And we'd be in pieces.

'Cut!'

Red cards were issued. Apologies were made. Josh and I solemnly swore that we'd no longer be up to no good. But then, as soon as we heard the word 'Action!', we were helpless with laughter again. One of us would snigger and that would set the other off. Even if we didn't hear each other, or look at each other, the bloody millipede would slide down the table and we'd be doubled over yet again.

'Cut!'

We were taken to one side and given a talking-to. 'Listen boys, you're wasting *our* time, you're wasting *your* time and most of all you're wasting Dame Maggie Smith's time. It's not respectful and we'll remove you from the set if you think this is all just a joke. Is that what we need to do?'

We shook our heads. We knew this was a terrible show of form. We desperately wanted to demonstrate that we were professionals. We returned to our places, chastened and determined to keep our involuntary fits of laughter under control. We focused on Dame Maggie, patiently austere at the head of the class. Josh and I were as serious as we could be.

'Action!'

Corpse.

'CUT!'

It was no good. We didn't want to laugh but we were incapable of stopping ourselves. We could sense each other's smirks. It was like being brutally tickled - painful, and yet we couldn't stop laughing. Chris Columbus and the rest of the crew were beyond a little frustrated at this point. How the hell were they going to shoot this scene when the two dumb Slytherins kept mucking things up for them, all because of a slippery millipede?

In the end, they took the animals away. Each scene is filmed from various angles and they decided that, since they principally needed shots of Maggie, and our role was to help her performance, we could ditch the menagerie. So that's what happened, all because of Josh and my mismanagement of the millipede.

I felt mortified about my behaviour and so I went up to Maggie afterwards and apologised. 'I'm so sorry, Maggie, I don't know what came over me. It won't happen again ...' She kindly waved my apology away. I suppose that, after several decades of mastering her art, she was hardly likely to be derailed by a couple of teenagers pissing about with wands and a millipede in her eye line. An actor of her experience is near bulletproof in that regard. And I don't think my behaviour compromised our relationship. On set she was stern but kind - much like McGonagall herself. Off set, at premieres and events, she was always incredibly friendly and accommodating. I remember my parents being desperate to meet her and her being very cool about it. All in all, a true national treasure. Someone to look up to. And that's coming from a Slytherin.

• • •

From time to time, it should be said, I got as good as I gave. In *Goblet of Fire*, there is a scene where Mad Eye Moody turns Draco into a ferret and then, having been told off by McGonagall, back into Draco. The script made it quite clear that, when re-transfigured into human form, Draco should be stark bollock naked as he runs, humiliated, across a crowded courtyard. I didn't give it much thought, beyond making the occasional gag that they might not have a camera lens wide enough. But as the moment arrived to film the scene, and they handed me a see-through thong that made me rather hanker after my Snowman Three costume, the reality of the situation suddenly dawned on me. 'We're really going to do this?' I asked, thong in hand, a hundred teenage extras looking on.

'We're really going to do this.'

'Now?'

'Now.'

I looked at the skimpy G-string. I looked at the camera crew. I looked at the extras and the ADs and the other cast members. And it was only when a few of them started sniggering that I realised the *bastards* had been winding me up the whole time. I'd been the butt of their joke, made to look a bit of an arse, but thankfully my derrière remained covered and my modesty preserved.

16

DRAMIONE

or

THE CHICKEN AND THE DUCK

Let me take you forward a few years to Santa Monica, Los Angeles.

Harry Potter is in my past. I'm living here in Venice Beach and in many ways it's the worst possible place for a person with any kind of public profile. Tens of thousands of tourists descend on the place every day, and Americans are not known for their shyness when it comes to approaching people they recognise. Somehow, though, I get away with it. Maybe it's because I spend most of my time in the same pair of wet swimming shorts I've been in all week, sporting a backwards baseball hat, skating beside the pier. Even if somebody does recognise me, they'll likely shake their heads and think, *That* can't *be Draco, he looks too much like a beach bum.*

But there's celebrity, and then there's *celebrity*. As I'm reminded when Emma Watson comes to hang out.

I suggest we go out for the day. It sounds like a small thing, right? Just a day hanging out on the beach with an old friend. But it's not a small thing for Emma. I'm not sure it's something that Emma would ever really do without some encouragement. And you can see why, the moment you step out of the door.

I'm wearing a T-shirt that says 'Women Do It Better', much to Emma's approval. She wears sporting joggers and a T-shirt, a world away from the red-carpet Emma that everyone knows. Still, the very first person we see turns her head in recognition. Emma still looks almost exactly how she did when we finished filming the Potter films. She certainly doesn't look like a beach bum. Looks like our chances of travelling incognito are zero.

Holding on to each other, we ride my electric longboard along the boardwalk. A Mexican wave of faces turns as we pass. At first people are astonished. Then they're excited. They shout Emma's name. They shout Hermione's name. Eventually they start to chase us along the boardwalk. We head to Big Dean's for a pint. I'm a regular here. Pretty much all the staff are friends of mine. But suddenly it's like they've never seen me before. All eyes are on Emma. One of the staff even approaches her with a CD of his music in the hope that, as a 'famous person', she can pass it on to someone influential.

Emma takes it all in her stride. She's had this kind of reaction since she was a teen. I was able to live something of a normal life alongside my Hogwarts career, but for Emma that was near impossible. She's had to learn how to deal with it. We leave the bar and head back along the beach, where we hide under an old lifeguard stand, two on-screen enemies now closer than ever, taking respite from the constant glare of public attention. As we sit there we think back over the years to a time when life was different, when Emma was not nearly so comfortable being the centre of attention and I was not nearly so attentive as a friend.

• • •

My relationship with Emma Watson did not start well. First off, there was my cold retort at the first Potter audition, when I gave a frizzy-haired nine-year-old both barrels of my on-set world-weariness. She'd have been forgiven for not wanting much to do with me.

It got worse.

There was a definite Gryffindor/Slytherin divide in the early days. Two cliques that kept their distance from each other, largely because we didn't spend that much time working together. Daniel, Emma and Rupert were one clique. Jamie, Josh and I were the other. We weren't unfriendly to each other by any means, but we were just different somehow. The main three were squeaky clean. We weren't. The main three came from well-educated backgrounds. Sure, I hardly had a rough life, but there was a definite difference to our respective upbringings. I suppose we thought we were a bit cooler. We'd spend our free time together listening to rap music - Wu-Tang, Biggie, 2Pac - so when word reached Josh and me that nine-year-old Emma had put together a little dance show in her dressing room that she wanted to present to us at lunchtime, we were predictably dismissive. Going to a dance show over arguing which rap style was best, East Coast or West Coast? Weak, bruv.

We sniggered our way down to Emma's show, and the sniggers grew louder as she danced. We were just being shitty boys, largely out of awkwardness and because we thought taking the piss was cool, but Emma was visibly upset by our thoughtless reaction. I did feel like a bit of a dick, and rightly so. In the end, though, it was up to one of the hair and make-up ladies to tell me what was what. 'She's very upset,' she said. 'You shouldn't have laughed at her. You need to apologise.'

I *did* apologise and Emma accepted my apology. Everybody moved on. It was just a stupid, teenage act of thoughtlessness, the sort of thing that happens every day. So why does that moment stick in my memory? Why is it so painful for me to recall?

The answer, I think, is that I've grown to understand with the passing of the years that of all of us, Emma had the most to deal with, the most difficult situation to negotiate, and from the earliest age. She would become one of the most famous women in the world - and to my mind one of the most impressive - but it's easy for an outsider to see only the celebrity, and not take a moment to consider the challenges that come with it. At the start, Emma wasn't thirteen like me, or eleven like Daniel. She was nine. There's a big difference. She'd never been on a film set before, and out of the lead child roles she was the only girl. She was surrounded by 'boy humour' - silly practical jokes and pre-pubescent laddishness - and while she more than held her own in that respect, and could even be cheekier than the rest of us put together, it can't have been easy. And the pressures she experienced went further than just having to deal with stupid boys. Emma was never afforded a normal childhood. She was in many ways treated like an adult from the day she was cast. It's a phenomenon that can, I think, be more difficult for girls than for boys. They are unfairly sexualised in the media and beyond. They are judged on their appearance, and any hint of assertiveness raises an eyebrow that wouldn't happen if it came from a guy. I wonder what would have happened if somebody had the ability to look into the future and tell the nine-year-old Emma what it held. That this thing she'd signed up for would be with her for the rest of her life. That she would never be able to get away from it. That she would be hounded forever. Would she still have done it? Maybe. But maybe not.

So the last thing she needed, in an environment that should have been - and normally was - safe and friendly and familial, was Josh and me laughing at her dance. That's why I feel ashamed by the memory of our behaviour. And that's why I'm glad that our friendship did not founder on the rocks of my insensitivity, but became something deeper. A touchstone for both of our lives.

• • •

I've always had a secret love for Emma, though not perhaps in the way that people might want to hear. That isn't to say there's never been a spark between us. There most definitely has, only at different times. A lady called Lisa Tomblin was in charge of hair on the later Potter films. I'd known her from the age of seven, when we'd worked together on *Anna and the King*, and it was she who first told me that Emma had a crush on me. She was twelve, I was fifteen. I had a girlfriend, and in any case, I'd been programmed to dismiss any talk of that kind of stuff. I laughed it off. In fact, I don't think I really believed her.

But time passed and things changed. We grew closer and the more I saw and understood what her life was like, the more empathy I had for her. I became very defensive of her, whenever she needed defending. I began to see her not as a little girl, nor as a public-property celebrity, but as a young woman who was doing her very best to negotiate a life where ordinary social situations and interactions were practically impossible. From time to time I think it was incredibly difficult for her. Occasionally, I imagine it must even have felt overwhelming. Some people just didn't understand that. They failed to appreciate the pressures of being in the spotlight from such an early age.

Most of the time in those early days, though, if Emma seemed unforthcoming it was not because she was having an off day, but for more complex reasons. When we were filming *Prisoner of Azkaban*, we found ourselves in the middle of a forest in Virginia Water to shoot the scene where Buckbeak the Hippogriff attacks Draco. There were maybe fifty members of the cast and crew, including Daniel, Emma and Rupert, along with Robbie Coltrane and, of course, Buckbeak himself. It's not easy, when you're filming with that number of people, to keep under the radar. And since this was a public place we soon attracted the attention of some fans. Emma's instinctive reaction was to look away, to avoid eye contact and keep her distance while strangers shouted her name. It no doubt looked like standoffishness, like she couldn't be bothered to sign an autograph or interact with onlookers. The truth was, she was a twelve-year-old girl and she was terrified. I don't think she fully understood why everybody was so interested in her. It was hardly surprising, since we had little preparation from the studio about how to deal with such situations.

But I had a few more years under my belt and was a good deal less worried about interaction with the public. I took Emma to one side and tried to help her see that there was no reason to feel threatened, that it was perfectly fine to be friendly, that we had it in our gift to create a memorable moment for the fans who wanted to talk to us. Together we walked over and chatted to them, and I could see a weight lift from Emma's shoulders. Perhaps it went some way to making up for my thoughtlessness at laughing at her dance routine. Certainly David Heyman later told me that was one of the moments he saw I was growing up from an arrogant kid to a more thoughtful young adult. And I believe that it helped Emma come to terms just a little with the strangeness of the life she found herself living. In a way, we both helped each other grow somewhat that day.

Rumours started to abound that there was more to our relationship than we were letting on. I denied that I liked her in that way, but the truth was different. My girlfriend at the time knew straightaway that there was something unspoken between us. I remember using the familiar old line: 'I love her like a sister.' But there was more to it than that. I don't think I was ever *in* love with Emma, but I loved and admired her as a person in a way that I could never explain to anybody else.

One time we met up outside of Hogwarts - something that I rarely did with anybody else from the cast or crew, because I preferred to return to the ordinariness of my day-to-day life. I picked her up and we went for a long walk round a lake close to my home. Emma spent a good deal of time reprimanding me for smoking, then she suddenly told me something that will always remain with me. 'I've always known I was a duck,' she said, 'but I've spent my whole life being told I was a chicken. Every time I try to say "quack" the world tells me that I have to say "cluck". I even started believing that I *was* a chicken and not a duck. Then we started hanging out and I found somebody else who quacked. And that's when I thought: *To hell with them, I really* am *a duck!*'

Did I mention that Emma Watson has a way with words?

To anybody else, Emma's story about the chicken and the duck might have sounded like gobbledegook. Not to me. I understood exactly what she meant. She meant that we were kindred spirits, that we understood each other and that we helped each other make sense of ourselves and of our lives. We've been quacking ever since. I know for certain that I'll always have Emma's back, and that she'll have mine too.

And trust me, Emma's a good person to have looking out for you, not least because she has a mean right hook, as I found out to my detriment one day.

We were filming *Chamber of Secrets* when the *Prisoner of Azkaban* book came out. True to form I was one of the very last members of the cast to read it, but word reached me that it included a scene in which Hermione gives Draco a well-deserved slap in the face. Cool, this should be fun! I was very into my Jackie Chan films at the time, and was stoked to learn that Emma and I might have to indulge in some on-screen violence when we shot the next film the following year. So as soon as I heard this, Josh and I went to find her so we could practise our stage-fighting. There was a holding tent just off set - a bit like a wedding marquee. This was where we kids could hang out when we didn't have to be on set or in tutoring. To start with it was amply stocked with chocolate, crisps, Coca-Cola and - believe it or not - Red Bull, which I mischievously encouraged the younger kids to indulge in. It was free, after all. That soon changed when the mum of Matthew Lewis, who played Neville Longbottom, made the not unreasonable observation that me feeding unlimited chocolate and energy drinks to nine-year-olds was not the best idea in the history of ideas. Once again, my reputation with the chaperones was consolidated. The snacks, to our disappointment, morphed into fresh fruit and water and the holding tent became a tad less inviting. But it did have a ping-pong table and Emma, being a mean ping-pong player, was often to be found there.

Josh and I burst into the holding tent. Sure enough, Emma was hanging out there with another girl playing ping-pong. My imagination was sparked by the thought of enacting the perfect Jackie Chan stage slap, where the cameras are perfectly lined up from behind me to make it look as if her palm has made solid contact with my face, and I really sell it on screen even though Emma hasn't even touched me. Not even close. So I approached with an abundance of enthusiasm.

INT. THE HOLDING TENT. DAY.

Tom *and* Josh *hover around the ping-pong table waiting for* Emma *to crush her opposition. She looks somewhat perplexed by the manic glint in their eyes.*

TOM

Do you want to practise slapping me?

EMMA

(brow furrowed)

Excuse me?

TOM

Because in the next film, that's what you do. You slap me.

(lying through his teeth)

I just read it!

EMMA

OK, great.

TOM

(mansplaining)

Right. So. Here's what you do. You need to stand there, you need to use your body, you need to put everything into it to sell it, you need to …

While Tom *is talking,* Emma *calmly sizes him up, raises one hand and – not realising that he was talking about a stage slap – cracks him as hard as she can across the cheek.*

Beat.

EMMA

Like that?

Tom *blinks. Heavily. He's holding back tears.*

TOM

(in a clipped voice)

Great. Yeah. That's good. That's … great. Well done. Nice one. See you later, yeah?

He turns his back on Emma and sheepishly exits the tent, his tail firmly tucked.

I didn't have the cojones to tell Emma that I hadn't meant her to thwack me in the face, or that she nearly had me in tears. She didn't find that out till much later on. And when, the following year, we came to filming that scene, you can imagine my hesitation when they told me the slap had been rewritten into a punch. I pleaded with Emma to make very sure she was keeping her distance for our stage punch. I don't mind admitting that my cheek twinged at the memory of Emma Watson's previous right hook.

Emma has taught me so many valuable lessons over the years, most importantly: don't always follow the herd, never underestimate the power of a woman and, whatever you do, keep quacking.

17

THE WEASLEBEES AT WORK

or

GOLFING WITH GRYFFINDORKS

There were times when we kids were shepherded back and forth from set in a big bus. Imagine a regular, rowdy school trip, except the passengers are decked out not in their school uniform, but in wizard robes and wands. I'm thirteen years old and some of my Harry Potter wages have purchased me a portable CD player and a Limp Bizkit CD. I'm sitting on the bus next to Rupert Grint, their track 'Break Stuff' blaring over my headphones.

Maybe you know Limp Bizkit. If so, you might reasonably be of the opinion that it's not completely suitable for thirteen-year-olds. The themes are adult, the language is fruity. It was right up my street. I glanced to my right, where Rupert was quietly minding his own business. It occurred to me that I might be able to get him to break out into a full-blown Ron Weasley expression of bemused astonishment. So I took off my headphones and put them over his ears. His brow furrowed. His eyes widened. And as he heard the full wallop of Limp Bizkit's lyrics, that classic Ron expression spread over his face. You know the one. I might as well have dropped a spider in his lap.

When I remember that incident, I'm reminded of two truths. One is that there was a reason why most of the chaperoning mums had a moment or two when I was not their favourite person. Remember the skateboard? Remember the Red Bull? I was, I think, an occasionally disruptive influence on some of the younger kids, whether by distributing sweets or exposing their sons and daughters to the more explicit side of American rap music. The other is that the actors who played the Weasleys were everything that you wanted them to be in real life: funny, kind and laid-back. And none more so than Rupert.

• • •

I had, of course, met Mark Williams, who played Mr Weasley, when I was filming *The Borrowers*. On Potter, we rarely saw each other. Our scenes tended not to coincide, so my contact with him was limited to premieres and press junkets. But those early memories I have of him, pre-Potter, recall an actor who was forever larking about. He was relaxed on set and keen to make everyone around him feel similarly relaxed. He always seemed to be the first to acknowledge that we were not doing anything particularly important - we were just making films - so it was okay to have fun in the process.

Mark was the perfect counterfoil for Julie Walters, who played Mrs Weasley (much to my mum's excitement). While she was the queen of kindness on set, she also had a mischievous sense of humour and she and Mark were forever mucking around. They were both warm and incredibly down-to-earth. They were, in short, the perfect Weasleys. I'm sure they were a good part of the reason why Rupert, along with James and

Ollie Phelps who played Fred and George, had such a sense of fun on set. When the Weasleys were together, they were always relaxed and having a good time.

On screen, Rupert and I were bitter enemies. Off screen I had, and have, nothing but love for the Ginger Ninja. It was almost impossible not to feel that way. From the very beginning he was always completely hilarious. This is the guy who got the part after sending in a video of himself rapping the immortal line 'Hello there, my name is Rupert Grint, I hope you like this and don't think I stink.' He was, unsurprisingly, extremely Ron-like. He was incredibly cheeky, with a habit of blurting out vaguely inappropriate comments that most people would have suppressed. He had a massive - and quite expensive - problem with laughing on set, thanks to Chris Columbus's red card system that cost him several thousand pounds. Corpsing on set is an occupational hazard for actors, especially young ones. All it takes is for somebody to say the wrong thing or to catch your eye in a certain way, and it doesn't matter how many stern words you receive, or how many legendary actors you are working with, it's almost impossible not to dissolve into fits of laughter each time the cameras start to turn. Of all of us, Rupert was by far the most susceptible to that.

Rupert always seemed entirely unbothered by anything. Despite all the pressures he's been under from day one of Potter, I've never heard him complain or appear to be even slightly pissed off with the occasional downsides of being in the public eye. He's just a good, sweet-natured person, seemingly able to take anything and everything in his stride. He's much less 'starry' than you might imagine an actor of his profile to be. And although the characters we played despised each other, off set I always felt we had a good deal in common. We both did the same thing with our wages: we enjoyed them, wholeheartedly. Go to either of our houses and you'll find crazy trinkets galore. I bought a dog, he bought a llama. Two, actually, which in a couple of years turned into sixteen (llamas mate enthusiastically, apparently). He bought a nice set of wheels, just as I did. But whereas I got myself a soft-top Beamer (roof down even in near-freezing conditions), he fulfilled a childhood ambition to be an ice-cream man by quietly spending his hard-earned on a fully loaded ice-cream van, which he spontaneously turned up to work in and started giving out free ice creams. He even used to drive round sleepy villages distributing ice creams to kids astonished at being handed a 99 by Ron Weasley in the flesh. It was crazy, but somehow entirely characteristic of Rupert. Despite everything, he didn't know how to be anything but himself.

Everyone changes a little as they grow up. As we were making the later films, Rupert became a little quieter and his playfulness became a little more reserved. But he never lost his authenticity or his gentle, genuine nature. And in later years, of all the friends I made on the set of Harry Potter, he's the one who has shared my passion for certain projects. For a number of Christmases now I've headed off to Great Ormond Street Children's Hospital in London to hand out presents to the kids who find themselves in hospital over the festive period. I start the day by going to Hamleys toy shop (yes, the one I used to go to after auditions with my mum) and do my best to blag as much Potter merchandise as possible. Then off to the hospital with a Santa sack full of toys. On one occasion, I texted Rupert the night before to ask him if he'd come along with me. It sounds like a small thing - it *is* a small thing compared to what some of those kids in hospital have to go through - but I was very aware that for Daniel, Emma and Rupert, more so even than for the rest of us, the question of charity work is a difficult one. We have the ability to help people simply by turning up. Sometimes, we don't even have to turn up at all. Daniel, for example, can sign ten photos and make thousands of pounds for a charity overnight. So while most people have a very good reason why they might not want to devote big chunks of precious spare time to charitable causes, our reasons are less convincing. It is, of course, a quiet privilege to do what we can for those less fortunate than we are, but that privilege comes with an uncomfortable question. Where do you draw the line? Where do you stop? There's no shortage of people in need of help and it would be easy to beat yourself up for not doing more. Like all of us, Rupert does what he can to leverage his profile for good causes, but it would have been quite understandable if my last-minute request for Great Ormond Street had been one request too many (not least because I know how it crushes him to see children who are not well). But, ever enthusiastic, he turned up the next day with his partner. No management team, no driver, no fuss: just modest, nonchalant Rupert, happy to give his time to brighten the days of some kids whose days sorely needed brightening.

That's Rupert in a nutshell: quirky, cheeky, thoughtful, reliable, kind - and a good guy to know if you fancy an ice cream.

• • •

Fred and George Weasley were played by the Phelps twins, James and Ollie. They're a couple of years older than me, so there was no chance of shocking them with a blast of gangster rap. It took me almost a decade to work out which was which and I certainly never risked calling them by their names, in case I got it wrong. But although we didn't find ourselves in many scenes together, we developed a friendship that endures to this day. Both are as warm and funny as their characters.

Give Fred and George an inch of fun and they'll take a mile of it. James and Ollie shared this trait with the fictional twins. They were always extremely good at making the most of any given situation. If there's a joke to be made, they'll make it. If there's something to blag, they'll blag it. When we were making the later films, the filmmakers wanted to shoot numerous 'behind the scenes' features as bonus material. They suggested going to everybody's houses and filming them going about their daily Muggle activities - walking the dog, washing the car, mowing the lawn and so forth. Mostly we were unenthusiastic about these suggestions. The Phelps boys had other ideas, and they had a very Fred and George way of 'suggesting' it. They played golf, as did Rupert, and I had also just started to enjoy hacking a white ball around. Why don't we all go to play golf somewhere iconic, they casually suggested, and they can film that? How about, say, the Celtic Manor in Wales, a very popular golfing destination that was about to host the Ryder Cup on their brand-new, impossible-to-get-on-to course?

Much to our delight they fell for it, and so James, Ollie, Rupert and I prepared to road-trip our way to the Celtic Manor. But hang on! Surely it wouldn't work if there were other golfers ahead or behind us, the twins helpfully pointed out. We would have a camera crew with us, who would only get in the way of other golfers. A brilliant idea seemed to arrive spontaneously. Wouldn't it be much more sensible if we were to have the whole course to ourselves, they said almost in unison. Their cunning observation was taken on board, and the upshot was that one of the most desirable golf courses in the world was booked out for a whole day, simply for the four of us to hack away at. As in every golfing contest we've ever had, the Weasleys won. Bloody Gryffindorks.

18

DRACO AND HARRY

or

TWO SIDES OF THE SAME COIN

Nobody knows - nobody can ever know - what it's like to be Daniel Radcliffe. There isn't a single person in the whole Potter project who had more pressure on him or her than Daniel. From the moment he was cast he was never fully allowed to be a Muggle kid. Not really. And while the same was true for Emma and Rupert, for Daniel the spotlight was just that little bit more intense. He was the Boy who Lived, after all, but he was also the boy who would never live a normal life. I had the privilege, like most ordinary teenagers, of being able to make some shitty decisions in my youth. The worst repercussions for me were having a Polaroid mugshot hung up on an office wall in HMV Guildford. For Daniel, the consequences of being a regular teenage hooligan would have been so much weightier. Almost from day one, people were taking pictures of him, secretly trying to record him, trying to catch him in a compromising or vulnerable position. At no point did he - could he - give them the opportunity to do so. The weight of the films rested almost solely on his shoulders.

I have such respect for the way he learned to cope with that pressure, and such love for him as a person. Of all the grand names I found myself surrounded by during my time on the Potter films, it's Daniel from whom I've perhaps learned the most, and in whom I see myself to the greatest extent.

Perhaps that seems strange, given that we were cast partly because of our similarities to the roles we played. Harry and Draco are enemies from the off, after all. But I don't see it that way. I would say Harry and Draco are two sides of the same coin, and I see myself and Daniel in a similar way.

We mostly kept our distance at first. Whenever we saw each other around set, we limited ourselves to a characteristically British nod of the head and a 'Morning, you alright? Sweet.' While I was busy larking around with the Slytherin lads, Daniel was busy being busy. Our paths didn't cross as much as you might imagine. When our paths *did* cross, what struck me about him was his fierce intelligence and almost savant-like memory for obscure cricket stats and *Simpsons* trivia. We'd sit on our broomsticks between takes while the crew re-set a scene, doing *Simpsons* quizzes, and nobody had a deeper knowledge of niche facts than Daniel.

As the films progressed we grew friendlier and started seeing each other a lot more. I'd go round to his house from time to time to watch the cricket, get a pizza and probably smoke too many cigarettes. (We were definitely two youngsters who were smoking before our time! A visitor to Leavesden would have a good chance, if they were to wander behind one of the dodgy old warehouses and look under a tower of scaffolding, of seeing Harry, Draco and Dumbledore huddled together against the cold, drinking tea and enjoying what we euphemistically referred to as 'a breath of fresh air'.) The more I got to know

Daniel, the more I saw how similar we were in so many ways. We're both hyper-aware of our surroundings and the emotions of others. We're both emotionally very sensitive, easily affected by the energy around us. It always seemed to me, and it still does, that if I had been an only child like Daniel, free from the influence of three older brothers, I would have ended up a lot more like him. And if Daniel had enjoyed the wayward influence of Jink, Chris and Ash, it wouldn't surprise me if he'd have ended up a lot more like me. And there is a symmetry to that, because I think the same is maybe true of Harry and Draco. I would never have understood this in the early days of Potter, but as the films progressed it became increasingly apparent to me. And one of the reasons it became apparent to me, I see now, was Daniel's developing skill as an actor.

Daniel would be the first to admit that when we all started out none of us really knew what we were doing. Sure, he and I had been on film sets before, but how good can somebody that young really be? Daniel, however, wanted to get better from the get-go. He always looked back on his previous work with a bit of a frown, and he had the admirable quality of knowing he could cruise through the role on auto-pilot, but not wanting to. He cared, deeply, and from day one he set about becoming the very best actor he could be. Which is quite a task when you've been given the role of Harry Potter. In my opinion it was the hardest part to play. Harry is and always was the staple, the solid ground, the reliable character. He has to be like that for the rest of us to dance around him. Draco's aloofness, Ron's jokes, Hermione's sharp wit, Hagrid's bumbling kindness, Voldemort's wickedness, Dumbledore's wisdom: all of these are thrown into relief by Harry's constant, unwavering solidness. It takes a special kind of skill to achieve that solidness and still draw the eye and move the audience.

Daniel learned fast and learned well. He quickly became a very special actor. Maybe it was because he, more than any of us, was surrounded by brilliance and it inevitably rubbed off on him. Perhaps he had the kernel of brilliance in him to start with. Whatever the truth, he soon started to hold the attention of everybody around him whenever he was on set. It was inspiring for the rest of us. We followed his lead, and if ever there was a person you'd want to follow into battle, Daniel, like Harry, was him. He was great at reminding us, simply by the way he held himself, to take our opportunity seriously, while having a lot of fun doing so.

Even if I didn't always follow Daniel's lead in that respect, his conscientious attitude eventually rubbed off on me. I learned more from watching and acting alongside him than I did from any of the adults. When the time came for Draco to develop as a character, if I had any success at all in portraying that development, it was in part thanks to watching Daniel.

Draco's development was not something I gave a great deal of thought to during the early films. We establish in *Philosopher's Stone* that he's the slimy git. In *Chamber of Secrets* we see something of his privilege: he gets the best broomstick and effectively buys his way onto the Quidditch team. He's the kid at school whose dad buys him a Ferrari for his first car. He doesn't seem to have an ounce of humanity, but although the whole Muggle world learns to dislike him, there is no sense of his snottiness snowballing into something worse. As a result,

I mostly spent the first five films standing in the corner sneering. I didn't need to think too much about Draco's development, because there wasn't any. He was always the same.

Then, in *Harry Potter and the Half-Blood Prince,* everything changed. Through Draco, we see that the bullies are often the bullied. Very early in the shoot the director, David Yates, took me to one side. 'If we can just get one per cent of empathy towards Draco,' he said, 'we'll have succeeded. Remember that you're planning to do the worst thing that's ever happened in the wizarding world: kill Dumbledore. When you hold that wand, it's the power of holding an army in your hand. We need to feel for you. We need to think, he had no choice.'

Draco Malfoy was the boy who had no choice. Dominated by his overbearing father, coerced by the Death Eaters, cowed into fear of his life by Voldemort, his actions were not his own. They were the actions of a boy whose agency has been ripped from him. He could not make his own decisions, and the turn his life had taken terrified him. The scene in which this became most apparent was when Harry comes across him crying at the sink, before they duel and Harry uses the *sectum sempra* spell. It was one of the few scenes Daniel and I performed just the two of us, and I felt unfairly praised for it. For me, the genius was in the writing. But if I did manage to raise my game to follow Draco's development, it was in large part down to what I'd learned from watching Daniel. I couldn't get away with being the boy sneering in the corner; I had to find a way to put meat on the bones of the character.

For me, Draco's arc in the final films gets to the very heart of one of the main themes of the Harry Potter stories: the theme of choice. It's an arc that reaches its climax during the scene in Malfoy Manor. Harry is disfigured. Draco is called upon to identify him. Is this Harry Potter, or is it not? There was no discussion on set about whether Draco knows for sure if this is Harry. My opinion is that he knows *exactly* who it is. So why doesn't he say so? The reason, it seems to me, is that the boy who had no choice finally gets one. He can choose to identify Harry, or he can choose to do the right thing. At every moment up until then, he'd have dobbed Harry in. Finally, though, he understands what Dumbledore told Harry early in the story: that it's our choices, not our abilities, that show us what we truly are.

That's why I see Harry and Draco as two sides of the same coin. Harry is the product of a family who love him so much, they are prepared to die for him. Draco is the product of a family who bully and abuse him. But when they have the freedom to make their own choices, they reach a similar destination.

19

A BOP ON THE NOSE

or

CRABBE, HAGRID AND THE SPOOKY RUBBER TOM

There were hundreds of actors on the Harry Potter set. Some I barely - or never - saw. Others I got to know well. So let me take you on a little tour around Hogwarts, and I'll introduce you to a few of the faces.

• • •

I've told you about Emma Watson's right hook. Long story short: keep away from it. But she wasn't the only one to plant a knuckle sandwich on my cheekbones. And from time to time, I gave as good as I got.

Devon Murray played Seamus Finnigan. He was always brilliant on set and a proper little Seamus. He was a real motor-mouth and mischievous, but kind. He clocked me in the face once, in a department store when we were on location. I can't remember why. Maybe I'd made some sarcastic comment. Maybe I was completely innocent and it was just the result of a dare. We used to get up to all kinds of nonsense like that. I remember somebody making a rancid potion of Coke, milk and coffee beans and offering a quid to anyone who would drink it. So perhaps, in a similar vein, somebody had offered him fifty pence to deck me. It wasn't personal. At least, it was as impersonal as a punch in the face ever can be.

Jamie Waylett, who played Crabbe, once received a childish bop on the nose in the Great Hall from me. That wasn't personal either. It was just standard behaviour for the three Slytherins, who were thick as thieves. Josh 'Goyle' Herdman was about my age, but Jamie was several years younger. It didn't stop us from being close, because Jamie was way older than his years. Like me and Josh, he was very into hip hop and was an extremely talented rapper. But there was sometimes a sense that he carried round with him a kind of pent-up aggression. We were close, but we fought. In that sense, I suppose, we were in real life very much like the characters we played. Mostly it was childish over-exuberance. He'd antagonise me for something or other, I'd bite back and the situation would deteriorate. We had lots of scenes together, which meant we had lots of downtime together. And you know how it is when kids rub each other up the wrong way when they've been spending a lot of time with each other. But the next day it would be as if nothing had happened. We were just kids being kids, albeit lairy ones.

One day, though, we were filming in the Great Hall. Jamie was sitting to my left at the Slytherin table, Josh to my right, and Jamie was winding me up incessantly. There was no malice in it, and on another day it might have been me needling him, or Josh needling me. Jamie kept kicking me under the table and elbowing me and whispering under his breath that I was a twat, just as the cameras were starting to roll. Now, I was not entirely innocent when it came to messing around on set, but I did *try* to be professional. I did *try* to be conscientious. One of the things that the adults really hammered into us was that once the crew had spent hours setting up a shot and the cameras were about to roll, whatever it is that you're doing, you shut up and wait to hear the magic word: 'Action!' And just because the camera isn't pointing at you, it doesn't mean you don't have to act. In fact, your acting off camera can sometimes be as important as your acting on camera. Your reactions, your eye line and your dialogue are ballast for whoever is on camera at the time. For whatever reason, I found Jamie's needling particularly irksome that day, so a millisecond before they called 'Action!', I turned and punched him straight on the nose. Not hard, but enough to make his nose leak a little claret. Somehow it was Josh who got pulled up in front of the producers and given a lecture about not riling Jamie. Talk about crossed wires. Sorry Josh, mate.

When we weren't indulging in fisticuffs, though, Josh, Jamie and I were intensely close. We were normally getting up to some sort of mischief. When we weren't, we would be indulging our passion for music. I set up a little studio in my trailer and we recorded quite a number of tracks. It was about as hardcore gangster rap as three white English Slytherin boys could spit out. The recordings still exist. Crabbe and Goyle's lyrical skills still astound me, and I listen to them to this day.

As the films progressed, though, it became clear that Jamie's interest in filming them started to decline. He seemed to lack enthusiasm, to be despondent even. He pulled the same trick that I used to at school, putting his headphone cable up his sleeve and listening to music when he should have been listening to the director. It was an attitude that suited his character perfectly, since Crabbe doesn't give a monkey's about anyone or anything. But it became apparent to us who knew him that he was not having an easy time of it during filming, or even a particularly enjoyable time.

And then things started to become complicated for him outside of the world of Potter. After we'd finished filming *Half-Blood Prince*, he had a scrape with the law. It was hard, after that, for the filmmakers to invite Jamie back for the final films. I felt for him. He'd been there from the beginning and, scuffles aside, we'd been mates. It was part of his character not to care about authority, but when that characteristic informed his own life, there was suddenly no place for him. I understood the reasons, of course, but it was sad. Our original Slytherin trio was no more.

• • •

Robbie Coltrane, who played Hagrid, was one of the few actors I recognised when we started making the Potter films, thanks to his roles in *GoldenEye* and *Cracker*. Perhaps more than anybody else, he understood the importance of keeping it lighthearted. He was a joker, but he was also the person that the jokes happened to. Or rather, he was the person who allowed the jokes to happen to him, and his reactions were priceless. There was a phase when Daniel's and my hilarious on-set gag was to go around changing the language on people's phones so that it was difficult to find your way back to the English setting. Robbie was definitely the butt of that joke several times, because his reaction to it was so enjoyable.

He'd narrow his eyes, peer around and mutter: 'What fucker did that?' He acted as if he was ready to kill the culprit, but really he was just entering into the spirit of things. Robbie was always keen to remind us that we weren't there to cure cancer. We weren't saving the world. We were simply making a film. We should remember that, not get too big for our boots and try to have a laugh along the way. He had a good dose of Hagrid in him: the big friendly giant who never lost sight of what was important in life.

In the *Prisoner of Azkaban* scene where Draco is kicked by Buckbeak, he has to be carried off by Hagrid. All sorts of crafty technical wizardry was employed to make Hagrid look like a giant. Most of my scenes with him were not played by Robbie, but by Martin Bayfield, a six-foot-ten rugby player in an enormous animatronic suit. (It was an incredibly hot costume to wear. Jamie and I were often told off for corpsing at the sight of steam coming out of Hagrid's ears.) In this scene, however, Hagrid's face was fully on display, so rather than make him very big, they had to make me very small. They created a dummy Draco about a quarter smaller than my actual size for Robbie to carry. This was no toy - it took months to build and cost tens of thousands of pounds - but naturally, like any kid, I was delighted by the idea of having a fake mini-me to play around with. My immediate plan was to take it to a car park, wait for someone to reverse and then throw it behind the car. Somehow I managed to restrain myself from carrying out that practical joke, but my mum was on set that day and I did take special pains to freak her out with the spooky rubber Tom. Robbie joined in the fun. The more my mum squirmed at the thought of her youngest son immortalised in mannequin form, the more Robbie waved the decoy Draco in her direction, to the absolute hilarity of us all. That was Robbie through and through. He had a cutting sense of humour as an adult, but he was brilliant with the kids, too. (The dummy Draco is now happily retired and living out the rest of his days at the Potter studio tour at Leavesden.)

Robbie was also kind, and caring. In the first film, Hagrid takes Harry, Ron, Hermione and Draco into the Forbidden Forest. Part of that scene was shot in the studio where they built the Forbidden Forest. Part of it, though, was on location and required a night shoot. I have a distinct memory of sitting on a plastic tarp on the floor at two in the morning in a cold forest with Daniel, Rupert and Emma. Emma was only nine years old and she was curled up asleep next to me while we waited for them to set up the next shot. But while everybody was frantically going about their business, it was Robbie who kept spirits high and made sure that we were comfortable and warm and well looked after.

In later years, my main contact with Robbie would be on press junkets and publicity tours. He's a real petrol head with a vast knowledge of mechanics, motors, cars and planes. We shared that passion, but most of all I always looked forward to publicity appearances with him because you were guaranteed a lark and a laugh.

• • •

Let's face it: Neville Longbottom was never intended to be the stud of the show. Matthew Lewis, who played Neville from the beginning, very much looked the part in the first film. He had the ears, he had the face, he had the endearing accent. He was Neville head to toe.

But there was a problem. Each year, when we all congregated to make the next film, Matthew was ever so slightly hunkier, which meant that - physically speaking - he was ever so slightly less Neville-like. Fortunately he's a very good actor, but it reached the point in the later films where they had to give him a wedge behind his ears, fake teeth and a little fat suit to stop him looking like the hunk he was becoming. Who'd have thought that Neville would end up in his pants on the front cover of *Attitude* magazine?

Matthew is a great example of everything good about Potter. He's a lovely, down-to-earth guy, humble to a fault. His knowledge of and interest in all manner of subjects guarantees great conversation, and that makes him one of my favourite people to have a pint with. Like me, he prefers not to watch the films back (nobody likes hearing their own voice on tape, right?), but he's developed into a really impressive actor and has a quiet confidence in his own ability. Of all the Potter alumni I bump into, Matthew is one of those I enjoy seeing the most. Any Slytherin-Gryffindork rivalry is long forgotten.

• • •

There were certain actors on the set who you'd never really recognise out of character, even though they were absolute legends. They just looked - and I mean this in the nicest possible way - like slightly scruffy older men. John Hurt, who played Ollivander, was one of those. I'm a huge fan of his now, particularly of his performance in *Midnight Express*, but at the time

I had no idea he was one of the greats. You simply wouldn't know it to look at him.

The same was true of David Bradley, who played Filch. He was the very opposite of his character: there was nothing malevolent or bumbling about him at all. Whereas some actors demand attention whenever they're near the set, David was always unassuming. He'd sit quietly in the corner, the very model of calmness. But I learned a lot from seeing how he could morph repulsively into Filch, with such an expression of distaste and contempt. I always enjoyed watching his performance. He clearly loved his job.

I was on set one day when I saw another slightly scruffy older bloke wearing an old pair of jeans and a T-shirt. I'd occasionally seen him around and I thought he was one of the cleaning staff. What can I say? He just had that look. We were outside the Great Hall and I thought it would be a pleasant gesture to compliment him on his work. I squeaked my shoes on the polished concrete floor, gave him a thumbs-up and said, 'Top work, mate!' He turned around to see if I was talking to someone behind him, gave me a slightly odd frown and said nothing.

Later that day I was getting my barnet done and the same guy walked into the hair and make-up department. He seemed to be showing family and friends around. Bit weird, for one of the cleaning staff. I had a horrible feeling I might have made a faux-pas, so when he'd left I asked someone, 'Who is that?'

'Who?'

'That!'

They laughed. 'Gary Oldman, obviously.'

I cringed with embarrassment when I realised I'd mistaken him for the cleaner. I wanted to apologise - not that he'd really have given a monkey's - but in the end I took the easier route of totally ignoring my mistake and pretending I'd known who he was all along. In my defence, for such a big star, he was hardly starry at all. He was unassuming and down-to-earth, likely to be seen making a cup of tea for everyone, rather than playing the room.

Just as Sirius became a father figure to Harry, I had the sense that Gary became something of an inspiration for Daniel, helping him to navigate the tricky path of growing up in the spotlight as well as hone his acting skills. They seemed to me to share a very similar sense of humour and approach to the other cast and crew. I think some of us - myself included - were a bit jealous of that bond. We could see that, in part thanks to Gary's influence, Dan was really starting to learn the craft better than any of us. Who better to have on your side in that respect than Gary Oldman?

• • •

Warwick Davis was another of the very few Potter actors I recognised at the start because I was a fan of the film *Willow* (now the name of my four-year-old, squirrel-obsessed, bottomless-stomached Labrador). He was there from the start of the first film, in which he played Professor Flitwick - one of several roles he would take over the course of the films. He was always quietly charming and fun with the kids. He became a dear friend of mine, and I had to admire his method of getting around set. Because of his height, it would take him longer to get around than the rest of us, even when we were kids. So he brought in a modified Segway to whizz around on. It was cut to size, so the label read 'egway'. It was quite a sight, seeing Flitwick or Griphook sail past with a nonchalant wave and a cheery comment. 'Morning, chaps!' But there's no doubt that we got used to unusual sights, surrounded as we were with the characters and paraphernalia of the wizarding world ...

20

A KIND WORD FROM DUMBLEDORE

or

A BREATH OF FRESH AIR

As everyone knows, we had two Dumbledores. Sir Richard Harris played the role in *Philosopher's Stone* and *Chamber of Secrets,* then when he sadly passed away, Sir Michael Gambon took on the part.

At the time I had no real idea of what a legend Richard Harris was, as I had very little to do with him. He only ever said two words to me. He took me to one side in between scenes just outside the entrance to the Great Hall, peered at me in a very Dumbledore kind of way, and said: 'You're good.' Nothing more than that. I don't think he meant to blow smoke, and I certainly didn't realise at the time that I was receiving praise from one of the greats. Did *I* think I was good? Well, I had a sense that I wasn't doing what everybody else was doing. Draco never wants to follow the crowd. If the rest of the students are standing *here,* he'll be standing *there.* When they're looking scruffy, he's looking perfect. When their top buttons are undone, his are firmly fastened (a trait that I hated at the time, because what self-respecting teenager wants their school uniform to be just so?). So the character meant that it was easy for me to stand out.

But was that the same thing as being good? Did I deserve those kind words from the original Dumbledore? Truth is, these matters are completely subjective. We all knew - Daniel, Emma and Rupert included - that we had a lot to learn. Sure, we knew not to look down the camera lens and we knew how to find our marks, but it was the quality of the actors around us that made us look half decent. Like anyone in any field of endeavour, however, I had my moments that went well and my moments that were best forgotten.

Tom's cockiness sometimes helped Draco come to life on screen, and sometimes it didn't. In *Chamber of Secrets*, when Harry and Ron have taken Polyjuice Potion to transform themselves into Crabbe and Goyle, they follow Draco to the Slytherin common room. Harry has forgotten to take off his glasses, which led to a nice example of Chris Columbus's genius. When Goyle explains that he's wearing glasses because he's been reading, I was asked to improvise what would become one of my all-time favourite Draco lines. After take three, Columbus appeared a little giddy as he had a lightbulb moment. He crept over to me excitedly, pulled me to one side and whispered a zinger into my ear. 'When he says he's wearing glasses because he's been reading, you say: "I didn't know you could read."' We shared a smile and that was the take that made the final film. I knew it would because Chris burst out laughing after calling 'Cut!'

The following scene, on the other hand, was not my finest moment on set. The three of us walked into the Slytherin common room, Draco leading the way reading the *Daily Prophet*. Draco had a fairly chunky monologue. I didn't know my lines at all that day and it cost them a good few hours of filming.

I received a very substantial reprimand from David Heyman, and a phone call was even made to my mum telling her that I *had* to know my lines, or else. They ended up printing out bits of the script and sticking them into the newspaper so that I could read them out. I doubt Richard Harris would have been massively impressed if he'd been in attendance that day.

As I became more experienced, I began to understand that the notion of being 'good' or 'bad' in a scene is more nuanced than most people imagine. You can act your socks off, but if you're not connecting with the other actors in the scene, you're not doing a good job, just like whacking a tennis ball as hard as you can doesn't make for a good game of tennis. There is no individual good or bad. It's about the ensemble performance, about context and interpretation and opinion. If Rupert had played Draco and I'd played Ron, would the films have been different, or better, or worse? Yes to all of the above. Everyone's going to have their own view.

So I remember that kind word from the original Dumbledore with warmth, but I also take it with a pinch of salt. Much of what I exuded in those early films was the cockiness of a kid who was comfortable in front of the camera. The compliment felt good, but I kept it in perspective.

• • •

I had far more to do with our second Dumbledore than with our first. Richard Harris and Michael Gambon were very different characters in real life. Richard Harris reminded me of my grandpa in many ways. He had a warm, quiet wisdom about him, so well suited for the part he played. Michael

Gambon was more of a showman. He might have played the old wizard, but he was very much a young boy at heart. He was self-deprecating, but was at that age and stature that he could say almost anything and get away with it, however outrageous. He loved a funny story or a quick joke, and I think that comes across in his interpretation of the character. He gave, in my opinion, an incredibly impressive performance, especially in *Half-Blood Prince*.

Most of all, he was a lot of fun. One of the cardinal rules during filming was that you were never allowed to drive yourself to work. I think there were insurance reasons for this, but much more importantly the production people knew that half their cast would be late if they didn't have a driver sitting outside the front door at six-thirty in the morning, ready to take them to work. Not what you want when you're trying to herd thirty people onto set at the same time. There's an exception to every rule, however, and in this case Michael Gambon was it. He was a car guy - he had a brand-new Audi R8 at one point, and later a Ferrari. He'd drive himself into work and park the motor right outside Door 5, which was just about the most inconvenient place to put it. I'd be getting my hair dyed and I'd hear the revving of the engine outside. You'd best believe I was up out of that seat and running outside to check out Gambon's car with a head full of peroxide and silver foil. He used to let us kids sit in it, and although I'm sure he was breaking all manner of regulations, who was really going to argue with him? I mean, he is Dumbledore, after all.

Gambon liked to play dumb. He would often put on a pretence of confusion - 'What scene are we doing, darling?

Where are we? Which character am I again?' - but I'm sure he was largely winding people up. There were occasions when he had a less-than-complete grasp of his lines - they once had to be held up for him on massive boards behind the camera, which made me feel a little better about my own occasional shakiness in that respect. It didn't mean that he wasn't taken very seriously. He was, and particularly by me when the time came for us to shoot what was perhaps Draco's most significant and memorable scene: atop the lightning-struck tower in *Half-Blood Prince*. There were quite a few scenes in that film with Draco and just the adults, and this was the biggest of them. Draco has Dumbledore at wand-point and is summoning the courage to carry out Voldemort's instruction to kill the headmaster.

I wasn't exactly nervous about shooting that scene. I was excited. But I knew that this was my moment. I was used to coming in for rehearsals with all the other kids, but I'd never been asked in to rehearse by myself before. That changed for this scene, and I revelled in it. So much of my previous direction had been limited to: 'Loiter in the corner and look pissed off!', or 'Watch the tennis ball and imagine it's a dragon!' It felt good finally to have such a significant moment in the film, a piece that I could really put my mind to. So I rehearsed it well and I knew my lines backwards.

The big day arrived. For some reason, despite my preparation, I kept stumbling over a particular line. And it's a strange thing, but once you go down that particular rabbit hole, it's difficult to scramble back up. A little voice starts nagging in your head. 'You *know* these lines. You were awake all night reciting them. Why can't you get it right?' And once that voice starts nagging, there's no turning back - a bit like corpsing on set. We did three or four takes, maybe more, and on each occasion I messed it up. They called for a break, and Gambon magicked up a cigarette from out of his beard. He and I were often to be found outside the stage that housed the Astronomy Tower, having 'a breath of fresh air' as we referred to it. There would be painters and plasterers and chippies and sparks, and among them all would be me and Dumbledore having a crafty cigarette. 'Breath of fresh air, old chap?' he suggested.

We stepped outside, Gambon in his robes and the beard sock he wore (mostly to keep it straight but partly out of fear that he'd set it alight with his cigarette), me in my full black suit. We lit up, took a few puffs and then I apologised. 'I'm sorry, Michael. I do know the lines. I don't know why I keep messing it up. I'm just a bit all over the shop right now.'

He kindly waved my apology away but I was on edge and the apologies kept coming. 'Really, I don't know what's wrong with me. I don't know why I can't get the lines straight.' So he smiled and he said, 'Dear boy, do you have any idea how much they pay me per day? At this rate, if you keep fucking it up, I'll have a new Ferrari by next week.' He was absolutely deadpan, no hint of a joke. 'You keep doing what you're doing, son.'

Did he say that to calm my nerves? I don't know. But I do know that I instantly felt the pressure lift. We went back onto the set, and from that moment everything went swimmingly. For the second time, I'd received a kind word from Dumbledore. Michael Gambon's method of encouraging a less-experienced actor was very different to Richard Harris's, but it was effective.

You never know, until you see the finished film, how many of the scenes you've filmed are going to be in it. Sometimes there's almost nothing. It was gratifying to watch *Half-Blood Prince* because everything I shot made the cut. That's a good feeling. Had I lived up to Richard Harris's early compliment? As you know by now, I have reservations about stating whether an individual performance is good, because there are so many other contributing factors. Certainly I received lots of plaudits, but in truth, although I was pleased with the result, I felt unfairly praised. So much of the effectiveness of that scene derives from the way it was shot and where it lands in the story. From factors that were far beyond my control.

In between the time it took to shoot *Half-Blood Prince* and actually see it, I changed address. I'd moved out of my mum's house by now and was living in my own flat in Surrey, along with my beloved puppy Timber. My dear friend Whitey moved into my old flat. He called me one day to say a letter had arrived for me. I immediately assumed it was a parking fine, but he said he'd opened it by mistake. 'It's from some guy called Jo,' he said.

Some guy called Jo?

'And it's got an owl on the top of the page.'

The penny dropped. 'What does it say?' I demanded.

'I don't know. I haven't read it.'

'Well read it!'

'Something about a *Half-Blood Prince* ...' Safe to say, Whitey wasn't a fan.

'Just hold on to the letter,' I told him. 'I'm coming round now.'

That letter from Jo Rowling was the first contact I'd had with her for years. It was written on her beautifully gilded home stationery, said how pleased she was about how the film had turned out, and complimented my performance. Safe to say, that ended up in a frame and is still with me to this day. If it hadn't been for Michael's unorthodox pep talk during our breath of fresh air, however, it could have turned out very differently indeed.

lfonso introduces me to the Monster Book of Monsters.

HP3

eeting my favourite 'bloody chicken'
hile on location filming the Prisoner
f Azkaban.

Backstage on Broadway.

Me and Dan competing Quidditch and cricket.

With David Holmes after Slytherin clinches another victory.

A Comic Con in Japan

Off-set cuddles with Greyback.

The three Malfoys.

Better than hugging Voldy.

Weasley love.

A rare win for Gryffindor.

Slapsies on and off screen.

On the red carpet with Alan.

Quacking with my favourite duck.

Rise of the Planet of the Apes.

Jumping into Hollywood life

Skating to the beach.

Busking in L.A.

Meeting the fans.

Versions of myself

13 Hours

A United Kingdom

Labyrinth

Joseph Fiennes

Risen

Ophelia

Forgotten Battle

Beach life in California.

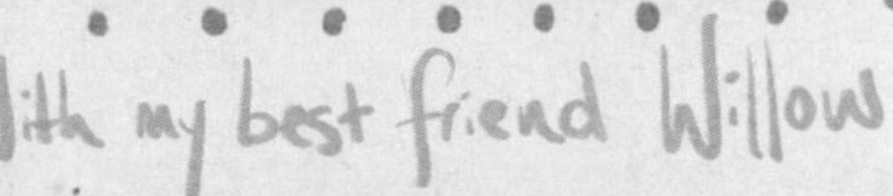

ith my best friend Willow

(She grew a bit)

Me and Greg Cipes in Venice Beach.

Enemies on screen make good friends off.

Beatriz Romilly Mandip Gill Sam Swainsbury

My West End debut.

21

ALAN RICKMAN'S EARLOBES

or

DON'T TREAD ON MY F*CKING CLOAK!

It's the sixth film, *Harry Potter and the Half-Blood Prince*. Snape has just killed Dumbledore. He, Draco, Bellatrix and an assortment of Death Eaters are marching through the Great Hall as they flee Hogwarts. We're talking high stakes.

David Yates, the director, has a vision: a V-shaped formation, Snape at the head, the rest of us fanned out behind him like bowling pins, or geese, as we storm down the aisle. Helena Bonham Carter has different ideas. She wants to dance along one of the long tables, kicking everything off, screaming and laughing maniacally. It's characteristically brilliant: Bellatrix comes across as being entirely unhinged. But we're having trouble nailing the shot for the rest of us. We do a couple of takes, sweeping quickly down the Great Hall with the camera team walking backwards in front of us. But it's not right. Alan Rickman is perfectly in focus, but the rest of us are a bit of a blur. We're too far behind him, that's the problem. David Yates directs us that we need to be closer to Alan.

From the very beginning, Alan Rickman had certain suggestions about Snape's costume. Snape would, he felt, have extremely long, flowing robes. These were to include a long cloak that draped along the ground behind him as he walked, like the train of a wedding dress. Once David had given us this new direction, Alan turned to the rest of us just before the cameras were about to roll. His eyes were narrow. His lips were thin. One eyebrow was ever so slightly raised. Any Hogwarts student, given the full force of that Snape-like stare, would have had legs of jelly. And I'm not going to lie, even we actors had an uncomfortable moment as we waited for him to say something. He spoke like Snape, each word distinct, heavy with meaning and punctuated by a long, agonising pause.

'Don't ...'

Silence. We glanced sidelong at each other. We wondered, *Don't what?*

'Step ...'

We looked down at our feet. Then we looked up at Alan again.

'On ... my ... fucking ...'

We blinked. We blinked again.

'Cloak.'

We gave a nervous laugh, but Alan wasn't laughing. He gave each of us a chilly stare, then he spun round, his cloak billowing bat-like behind him. Released from his glare, we Death Eaters looked at each other and one of us mouthed: 'Is he serious?' He was. *Deadly* serious. We were, on no account, to step on his fucking cloak.

We go for another take, bunched up closer this time. And who is it that's walking directly behind Snape? It's Draco, of course, and his feet will be just inches away from the trailing hem of the cloak as they march urgently through the Great

Hall. The director gives us our instructions. 'Chins up!' he says. 'Don't look down. We need to see your faces!'

Which means we can't keep a careful eye on the hem of Alan's cloak. So I give myself a good talking-to as we prepare for the take. *Don't tread on the cloak. Don't tread on the cloak. Don't tread on the ...*

'Action!'

Alan marches forwards. The rest of us follow.

One step ...

Two steps ...

Three steps ...

Now, Alan's cloak hung from his shoulders by means of a loop that went around his neck. When I inevitably stepped on the hem of his cloak, we'd barely reached the halfway point of the Great Hall. His head jerked back. For an awful moment I thought he was going to lose his balance. His strangled scream rang out around the set.

'Aaaargh!'

'Cut!'

Silence.

I gingerly moved my foot off the hem of the cloak. Alan turned. Slowly. I gave him my most apologetic smile.

'Sorry Alan,' I squeaked.

Alan said nothing.

'I ... I really didn't mean to do that,' I stuttered.

Alan said nothing again. He turned his back on me. *Shit,* I thought. *I've really pissed him off.*

A member of the crew shouted: 'Going again!' We returned sheepishly to our starting positions. I gave myself another talking to. *For fuck's sake, Felton. Don't tread on the cloak. Don't tread on the cloak. Don't tread on the ...*

'Action!'

This time round, you'd better believe I was making teeny-tiny steps behind Alan as the convoy of Death Eaters attempted their procession yet again. I made one teeny-tiny step ...

Two teeny-tiny steps ...

Three teeny-tiny steps ...

'AAAARGH!'

This time it was worse. Alan's whole body juddered backwards and he helicoptered his arms to keep his balance.

'CUT!'

Horrified, I looked down at my feet. Surely I couldn't have stepped on the hem *again*. To my eternal relief, I hadn't. One of my death-eating colleagues had overstepped the mark this time. And Alan was fuming.

'I'm not ...'

He announced.

'*Fucking* ...'

He declared.

'*Doing ... this ... again*!'

After some negotiation from the director, Alan agreed to give it one last try. The Death Eaters and I shared a glance of panic, but thankfully on the third take, no one stepped on his fucking cloak. However, if you think Snape looks a little strangled in that scene, now you know why.

• • •

In the following scene, Snape and the Death Eaters escape to the castle grounds. Hagrid's hut is set on fire. Harry and Snape do battle before Snape reveals that he is the Half-Blood Prince.

They'd built this exterior set at Leavesden: a massive hill, like a football pitch on a slant. We shot the scene at night. Helena was somewhere in the background being crazy, doing her dancing maniac bit having been mainlining espressos all night. Alan and I were standing in the middle of the field, waiting for Daniel to arrive.

There is a moment, when you're setting up a scene, that can sometimes be awkward. They'll be lining everything up and they'll put the actors in particular positions, and the actors will be required to stare at each other so that they can light the scene correctly. And then, between takes, while they're reviewing what they've just captured, it's the same deal: you're standing there like a lemon, patiently waiting for the call to go again. It's not always completely comfortable, gazing into the eyes of a person you don't necessarily know that well. I tend to use the earlobe trick: I'll stare at my colleague's earlobe instead of their eyes, which somehow eases the awkwardness and saves the moment for when the camera is rolling.

That evening, I found myself staring at Alan Rickman's earlobes. We'd done a take and were waiting for the director to review it. It seemed to be dragging on, and Alan and I were enshrouded by a long, awkward silence. At least, it was awkward for me. I always had the impression that Alan himself was never uncomfortable with silence. Silence, in fact, was his preferred state of being. And although by this point I'd spent years on set with him, I was still rather wary of the man. It hadn't helped that I'd stepped on his fucking cloak.

However, as we stood in the cold night air, I felt a typically British need to fill the silence. It shouldn't have been a big deal, but somehow it was. I eventually plucked up the courage to say, 'How's it going then, Alan? You alright? Feeling okay?'

Five long, silent seconds passed. Ten longer silent seconds passed. I started to wonder if he'd even heard me. Should I repeat my question? But then he slowly turned his head and fixed me with that Snape-like glare. I held my breath, wondering if I'd managed somehow to offend him. We listened to Helena shrieking in the background. The wind blew. It was cold, we were tired, and we weren't allowed to move from the spot where our feet had been planted for the last three hours. A Hollywood red carpet this was not.

Very slowly, very distinctly, Alan intoned, 'I've ... *peaked*.'

Then he turned his head to look the other way. But as he turned, I saw the whisper of a smile on his lips. And I realised then that, far from being the terrifying figure I'd always assumed he must be, Alan was a man with a brilliantly dry sense of humour. I didn't need to be wary of him. Far from it. I needed to relish the time I had with this smart, witty, interesting man.

• • •

At the beginning of filming, you were given your own chair with your character's name on the cloth back rest. These chairs would be with us for the duration of filming.

One day, Alan Rickman was sitting around with Helena Bonham Carter, Helen McCrory, Jason Isaacs and Michael

Gambon. Even by Harry Potter standards, that's a pretty impressive group of heavyweights. That's the crème de la crème of the British film world right there. They sat in their comfortable director's chairs. I had a much smaller fold-up chair, as when I started the films my feet would never have touched the ground from one of the taller ones. Almost immediately, Alan stood up. He walked over to one of the assistant directors, pointed in my direction and demanded that I was given a proper director's chair, so that I could sit at the same height as the rest of them. At first I wondered if it was a bit of a joke, but it soon became clear that he was absolutely serious. 'Alan, mate,' I said, 'it's fine, I'm happy sitting on my shorter chair.' He wouldn't take no for an answer. He didn't kick up a fuss, he wasn't impolite, he just quietly insisted that I was brought a chair of the same height as the others.

It was a small thing, but I'll never forget that moment of kindness. Alan wanted a younger cast member to be treated like an equal to these leading lights. He didn't have to do it, but the fact that he did spoke volumes about the man he was.

• • •

I think about that moment with the director's chair often, now that Alan has passed away. And not only Alan, of course. Richard Harris, John Hurt, Helen McCrory ... the list of actors from the Harry Potter films who are no longer with us inevitably grows. When I think of their passing, I find myself in purgatory because it's only now that I've reached adulthood that I've started to understand the effect that they had on me, and how brilliant they were as examples.

We barely notice the passing of time. There are moments when I still think of myself as the kid stealing DVDs from HMV. Then there are moments when I realise I'm definitely not. I'll meet fans who are closer to being unborn than they are to my age. In fact, most fans who approach me now weren't born when the first films were being made. I'll be on a film set where, far from being one of the scrappy kids, I'm the veteran. And it's in those moments, when it's important to me that I comport myself in the right way, that I realise what a positive influence those actors were, who I grew up with and who have gone on before. It strikes me that yet again life has mirrored art. In the Harry Potter films we played young, inexperienced wizards who went to a school to learn from brilliant wizards, and some of their brilliance rubbed off on us, so that seven years later we came out as half-decent adults. So it was in real life. The filmmakers picked a bunch of child actors, raw, unskilled and frankly without much idea of what they were doing. But if you let them hang around with the cream of the crop of British acting for a few years, they're bound to learn a thing or two.

And we did. But not in a clumsy way. Nobody took me to one side and said, 'Son, this is how you're supposed to behave on a film set.' I learned just as much from what these people *didn't* do as from what they did. They didn't demand special treatment. They didn't raise their voices or make a fuss about anything. It was much later in my career that I learned this is not always the norm. I've been on film sets, especially in America, where an actor will arrive an hour late on purpose, as a power move or out of sheer obliviousness. Where he or she will shout 'Cut!' in the middle of a scene when it is most definitely not their place to do so. It's the opposite to the calm, polite, prepared British authority my mentors exhibited. It always surprises me, when people comment on the way I hold myself on set, that anything less than basic respect for the people around me should even be considered acceptable. That's an attitude we learned from people like Alan. They are one of the main reasons, I think, that we kids didn't grow up to be assholes. We grew up watching them treat everybody on set with kindness, patience and respect. Alan would routinely offer to make cups of tea for people. He would talk to us children - and more importantly to every single member of the crew, from the camera team to the catering department - no differently to how he'd talk to his contemporaries. When he did make his presence felt - like when we trod on his fucking cloak - it was always with a subtle twinkle in his eye. Sometimes it could be hard to discern, but it was always there.

I wish, now that I'm older, that I could thank those actors who have passed away for everything they did for us. By their example, they kept us humble and good humoured, and I'll always be grateful for that.

22

UNDESIRABLE NO. 1 (PART 3)

or

THE WORLD'S BEST/WORST CHAPERONE

If you're a child on set, you need a chaperone. It's the law. And it makes sense. It's not easy to keep track of who's doing what when you have hundreds of children marauding all over the place. A chaperone is there to make certain you're safe, and to ensure that you're sticking to the many regulations that dictate what a child actor can and can't do during a day's filming, chief of which is timekeeping. They must ensure that you're never on set for more than three hours at a time and that your daily quota of tutoring is observed. Then they must check that you're eating properly, and that you're keeping out of trouble. Some of the rules seemed ridiculous at the time. They're even supposed to accompany you to the toilet, so they always knew if and when I was answering a call of nature.

Some of us - including Emma and Rupert - had professional chaperones. It was their job, and they were rigorous about ticking all the boxes that needed to be ticked and jumping through all the hoops that needed to be jumped through. Some kids had family members. Daniel, for example, had his dad Alan as a chaperone. I had my grandfather keeping a benevolent eye on me (as well as teaching me how to sneer), and I had my mum, who was used to accompanying me on film sets in any case.

And then, when nobody else could do it on *Prisoner of Azkaban*, when desperation kicked in, I had my brother Chris. He was, from a kid's point of view, the best chaperone I could have asked for. He was also, from an objective point of view, quite comfortably the worst chaperone in the history of filmmaking.

I've already told you about our habit of spending all night fishing before heading back to set and pretending that I was refreshed and ready after a solid eight-hour sleep. Chris taught me more during those all-night sessions than how to land a carp. He also taught the fourteen-year-old Tom how to roll a joint. Predictably enough, I soon graduated from preparing the joints to partaking of them. As I may have mentioned, having three older brothers meant that I progressed to certain activities earlier than some.

By the time Chris was my chaperone I'd moved from a dressing room to a trailer – a personal caravan in the parking lot, just outside Door 5. While I headed off to hair and make-up, he would eat his fill from the canteen and conk out in the trailer for the rest of the day. On those occasions, I'd never see him. I'd return to the trailer after a hard day's filming and Chris would be stretching and yawning and just beginning to think about getting up. He'd neck a cup of tea, chuff a few cigarettes, then we'd wrap up warm, head back to the lake and do the whole thing all over again.

A professional, fastidious, conscientious chaperone would literally be standing to one side with a stopwatch, ensuring that their charge's time on set had not overrun, or that their education was not suffering from a lack of time in the tutoring rooms. A professional, fastidious, conscientious chaperone would hurry their charge from set to lessons as quickly as possible. Not Chris. On the occasions when he was not having a kip in the trailer, we would saunter together from set to tutoring, taking the most indirect route across the studios, maybe stopping in at the kitchens for a can of Coke and a bar of chocolate ('Fill yer boots, mate, drink as much of that shit as you like!') and taking a few minutes for at least one 'breath of fresh air' behind the Great Hall.

The chaperone is the master, or mistress, of the per diem. This is a cash payment given to each actor, chaperone and crew member once a week to cover daily living expenses while we were away on location. Per diems amounted to about thirty pounds a day, and they were meant to be administered by the chaperone and spent on outgoings such as food, laundry and phoning home. Naturally, it would be madness to give the cash directly to the kids. Wouldn't it?

Chris didn't think so. Being the cool older brother, he was happy to hand over the dosh straight up. Sure, he wasn't above threatening to withhold the readies as a power card - 'Do as I say or I'll take your per diems away, maggot!' - but in general the cash went straight into my back pocket. And given that I could manage a whole day on a Peperami and a bag of McCoys, and that my desire to blow crisp twenty-pound notes on something as mundane as clean laundry was limited, my per diems went quite a long way on new skateboard wheels and the latest computer games. (Chris's per diems were also deployed in a way the filmmakers certainly didn't expect or intend: it was his weed money, and it enabled him to continue being a regular Harry Pot-head.)

Chris was also not beyond 'acquiring' the occasional memento from the set. I'm not saying it was entirely because of him that, on the final three films, they put in place spontaneous car checks for anybody leaving the studios. I'm not saying that they had to hire a whole security force on the back of some of his light-fingered shenanigans. There were plenty of regulars at Leavesden who would help themselves to a handful of Galleons or the occasional Hogwarts tie, but as far as offenders went, Chris was the Don. Certainly, several dummy copies of Gilderoy Lockhart's *Magical Me* miraculously apparated inside his bag. But he was not, I hasten to add, quite the cold-hearted criminal I'm making him out to be. The few things he took were eventually auctioned off, either for a local charity or for causes close to him. On one occasion he was offered a substantial sum of money to take secret pictures of the set so that they could be leaked before the next film was released. He declined, of course (at least he told me he did).

So, the worst chaperone but also the best. He treated me like an adult when I was still just a spotty teen. And he was definitely one of the most popular guys on set. Everyone liked Chris, and I think the experience was good for him. When he started on the films he was quite reserved and perhaps even looked a little aggressive, with his shaved head and two gold hooped earrings. Everyone on set welcomed him with open arms and that softened him up a little. He'd always been a bit brittle and dismissive about acting as a pursuit - unlike Jink, of course - but time with the Potter family helped, dare I say it, to bring out his more sensitive side. Bless his cotton socks.

• • •

As well as hardcore gangster rap and carp fishing, Chris and I were in love with cars of all shapes and sizes. We used to scan the pages of *Auto Trader* and salivate over potential acquisitions. We were obsessed with BMWs, black ones especially. No matter that I was far too young to drive at the time - Chris had his licence and I inherited his petrol-head nature, just as I had so many of his other enthusiasms. So when a black BMW 328i came up for sale nearby, and it turned out I had just enough cash in my bank account to buy it for my brother, there was no question in my mind that it would be a good way to deploy my earnings. We took a taxi to this guy's house and handed over a Tesco carrier bag full of used notes. Needless to say, he was a little suspicious. We sat there for ages, watching him count out the cash, holding each note up to the light while we forced ourselves to appear calm, as if we did this kind of thing every day. Once the guy was satisfied with his dosh, Chris took the keys and got behind the wheel with me at his side. With great restraint, he drove it slowly about 200 yards down the road and round the corner, out of sight of the previous owner. He stopped the vehicle. Engaged the handbrake. He turned to look at me. His face was hard to read. Then he grabbed my head in his two hands, kissed my forehead and let out a shriek of unbridled pleasure. I swear there was a tear in his eye. 'Thank you!' he said repeatedly. 'Thank you soooo much!' We both whooped triumphantly, as though we'd pulled off some great and elaborate heist. I was years away from being able to get behind the wheel of a car, but I was as obsessed with that BMW as Chris was. The wheels. The thunder of the engine revving. The face-melting acceleration. In most ways I was no different to a regular teenager with the obligatory Ferrari poster on his wall. The only difference was that in this case I had the means to turn mine and Chris's dream into a reality.

• • •

You may have twigged by now that the influence of the world's best/worst chaperone occasionally led me to express my more rebellious side. Chris introduced me to marijuana, the forbidden fruit, and it was of course referenced in every rap song I'd ever listened to. So it perhaps wasn't a total surprise that I should take his introduction to the Devil's lettuce and run with it. It led to perhaps my stupidest ever moment as a youngster.

The scene was a scraggly field behind the village hall in Bookham, Surrey, very near to where I lived with my mum. This was after my parents had divorced and I was going through a typical adolescent phase. Four of us were sitting in a circle on the grass. I was wearing my prized red Wu-Tang hoodie and we were passing round a joint. Joint-rolling paraphernalia was littered all around us: tobacco, rolling papers, a lighter, an eighth of hash. And the unmistakable, musty smell of weed hung over our little group.

It was as the joint was in my hand that I looked up and saw, less than a hundred metres away, two police officers, a man and a woman. They were walking in our direction with a certain purpose in their stride.

Shit.

One of my brothers - I shan't reveal which one - had given me a piece of advice for occasions such as this. 'Bruv, just remember: if it's not *on* you, they can't *do* you for it.' They had to prove, according to my legal counsel, that you were actually guilty of possessing the goods. If you didn't have the hash in your pocket, he told me, you were perfectly safe. With that advice ringing in my ears and the police less than fifty metres away, I stood up, resplendent in my bright red hoodie, gathered the paraphernalia in my arms and tried to force it, along with the joint, into a nearby hedge. I did this in plain view of the police officers as they continued their approach, before returning to my friends and sitting down again.

The police arrived. They looked down at us. We looked up at them with innocent eyes. The stench of wacky baccy made it absolutely obvious what we'd been doing.

EXT. A COMMUNAL FIELD SOMEWHERE IN SURREY. DAY.

POLICEMAN

What are you doing?

TOM

(full of piss and vinegar)

Nothing.

POLICEMAN

Yes you are. We just saw you put something in that hedge.

TOM

No, you didn't.

POLICEMAN

(patiently)

Yes, we did.

TOM

Nah, mate. Wasn't me.

There is a long, weighty silence. The police officers, eyebrows raised, are plainly not impressed by these cocky kids and their feeble legal strategy. And with each second that passes, the cocky kids look increasingly unsure about themselves. Until eventually…

POLICEMAN

Do you *really* want to go down this route, son?

TOM

(crumbling, the piss and vinegar draining out of him)

Sorry. No. Look, I'm really sorry, okay? I'm so sorry. *Please, I'm so sorry …*

They made me return to the hedge and recover the goods, which included the half-smoked, still-smouldering spliff.

Predictably enough, I was arrested for about a fiver's worth of hash. It was hardly the crime of the century. The police officers weren't exactly smashing a major international drug ring. Any other time, I think they'd have given us a rap on the knuckles and sent us home. But the policewoman was a trainee, and the policeman was showing her how to do things by the book. And so I was bundled into the back of a police van and the doors clanged behind me.

I was bang to rights. But the consequences of this latest brush with the law could have been much worse. I'm sure Warner Brothers had a certain amount of sway when it came to suppressing stories about their cast members being caught in compromising positions. But Draco arrested for being a pothead would have been a hard one to spike. As I sat in the van, though, I wasn't remotely worried about that. I wasn't remotely worried about anything because I was high as a kite. Then it hit me. Just as when I was collared in HMV, there was one thing that could make this sorry episode a whole lot worse. *Please,* I thought to myself, *please don't call my mum.*

They called my mum.

There's nothing worse than seeing the look of disappointment in your mum's eyes, especially when they're full of tears. We sat at a table in a little interview room at the police station. A uniformed officer came in, gave me a full-on *Line of Duty* interrogation, then proceeded to give me the bollocking of my life. I'm pretty sure they were just trying to scare me away from doing it again, but of course, once I'd sobered up to the humiliation of Mum's disappointment, I had to wonder: did they recognise me? If so, they were professional enough not to mention it. If not, I was glad, not for the first time, that I didn't have the same kind of profile as Daniel, Emma and Rupert. I was sent back home, tail tucked once again, feeling stupid. Happily, Warner Brothers never found out about my escapade (or at least they never told me they did). My days as Draco were not over.

23

MALFOY'S MANNER

or

A HUG FROM VOLDY

I've introduced you to my Muggle family. But one of the great advantages of being Draco was that it meant I had a second family: my wizarding, death-eating family. In the story, of course, no family could be more toxic than the Malfoys. To understand Draco, you need to understand that he's grown up with an abusive father. He never had a chance to become anything other than the unpleasant character he is, because he never knew any different. In real life, though, away from the story and the cameras, my Malfoy family became almost as close as my Muggle family. There's a reason why I still call Jason Isaacs, who played Lucius, Dad.

The first time I ever met Jason I was absolutely shitting myself. Chris and I had both watched him in *The Patriot* and we enjoyed how devilishly evil his character was. Our first scene was outside Borgin and Burkes, the dark arts shop in Diagon Alley. This was when we were making the second film, *Chamber of Secrets,* and I distinctly remember this lovely, charming man reaching out to shake my hand and introducing himself as my father. He was dressed as Lucius Malfoy, of course. However, he oozed none of Lucius's menace. He immediately took me under his wing, introducing himself to the cast and crew with me by his side and making me feel completely at ease. He offered to make me a cup of tea and run lines. He started to tell an anecdote that had people around him laughing from the start. As I was basking in the reflected glory of his storytelling, I heard the words 'Quiet on set!' I knew what that meant, but Jason continued with his story.

'Roll cameras!' I took a breath. Jason seemingly didn't.

'And ... action!'

Mid-punchline, he turned to look at me like he hated me – in a loving sort of way. Jason was gone. This was Lucius ...

There was something very discombobulating about seeing a person's character switch so suddenly and so completely. There was no acting required for me to appear instantly terrified of him. Maybe he did it by design, maybe not. Either way, it worked. Part of Lucius's costume was a black cane with two fangs at the end. It was Jason's idea that the cane should conceal his wand. When he first made the suggestion to Chris Columbus, Chris wasn't keen. But Jason persisted: 'I think it would be a really cool idea!' To which Columbus replied: 'The merchandise people are going to love you ...' The fangs at the end of that cane were a good deal sharper than either of us realised. During that first scene, he whacked me on the hand with them. I resisted tears and managed to ignore the physical damage and stay in character until the end of the scene, with Jason looking at me like I was a piece of shit. Then we heard the word 'Cut!' Lucius Malfoy dissolved away and Jason was back, full of apologies and concern. His thin-lipped 'Don't touch, Draco!' was replaced with a touching, concerned 'My darling boy, did I hurt you? Are you okay?' It was as if a switch had been flicked.

Even now I get goosebumps when I remember Jason's transformations. When he was Lucius, I never quite knew what to expect. Which angle was he going to whack me from this time? How would he direct his menace? From an acting point of view, it was a gift. His performance made sense of Draco. Seeing him treat me in such a way gave me licence to treat everyone else similarly, because it helped me understand that there were two sides to Draco's story: he was a bully, of course, but at heart he was a little boy who was terrified of his dad.

I grew to learn that Jason's ability to flick the switch was unique. Lots of the adult actors I worked with had little routines or vocal exercises that they used to break out of themselves and into character, whereas Jason seemingly had the ability to become Lucius at the snap of a finger. I've never met anybody quite so comfortable on a film set as him. It's almost like he was born on set. He talks to everyone, includes everyone, is forever in the middle of a perfectly told anecdote. And when the 'Quiet on set!' call goes out, and everybody starts to get ready for a take, you can be sure that Jason will still be in full flow, because he knows that as soon as he hears the word 'Action!', he can snap back into character without even a moment's thought. It is scarily impressive.

From day one, Jason treated me like one of his peers, an immediate equal, someone who he enjoyed talking to. (Whether that bit's true or not, you'll have to ask him.) When I was younger he looked out for me on set. As I grew up, he started to take an interest in my life, my passions, my music, my habits good or bad, and my career. He was never judgemental. He was the first adult I had met who spoke openly about growing up in the industry - the highs, the lows and everything in between. He offered advice about how I should set myself up for the future. I was a good actor, he told me. I mustn't waste my opportunity. I was a little taken aback by his encouragement, but it was gratifying to have that kind of support, and reassuring to have a person on my side who was so giving with his time and energy. If I can be half as present and helpful as he is on set in my career, I'll consider each project a job well done.

Have I said enough nice things about Jason now? Good. Because we took the piss out of each other as much as we enjoyed each other's company, and I can't let him get away with just unadulterated praise. He raised me better than that. Jason is not, shall we say, entirely free of the actor's traditional foibles. There was never anything shy or retiring about him. And there were times, of course, surrounded as we were with such strong acting personalities, that you had to work hard to make your presence felt.

One such occasion was when we were filming the opening scene for the final film, where Voldemort sits at the head of the table in Malfoy Manor, his Death Eaters in attendance and Charity Burbage floating in the air, about to be murdered. For me, that was a big scene. I was the only youngster, surrounded by so many great and experienced actors. A 'Make A Wish' child and his family visited the set before we started filming, and he excitedly handed Jason his copy of the book to be signed. Jason opened it up at the scene we were shooting to find that Lucius, in the original, has rather more to say than was written in the script. Jason was not one to hide his light under a bushel. His brow furrowed. 'Bloody hell!' he announced. 'I say this in the book!' He carried the kid's copy over to David Yates, the director. 'There's this line here!' he announced. 'I think it would be great for me to get it out there, don't you?'

David wasn't sure if he was joking. I still don't know if he was joking. Either way, a look of infinite patience crossed David's face. This was not the first time Jason had tried to adapt the script to give himself a little more screen time. David adopted a tone of gracious gratitude. 'Thank you, Jason. No really, thank you. What a *lovely* idea. But perhaps we could just do one as it's written in the script?' And a crestfallen Jason, well aware that he had just been politely refused, returned the book to the kid, who must have thought his precious copy had just been snaffled in quite a Malfoy-esque manner.

Joking aside, Jason became quite the role model for me. I admired his acting skills, of course, but I also admired his obvious devotion to his real family and was grateful for the friendship he offered me. In the years since Potter finished I have spoken to him more than anybody else from the films. It's a goal of mine to follow in his footsteps - but don't you dare tell him I said that.

• • •

As comfortable as Jason made me feel on set, another actor did quite the opposite. It didn't matter how many legendary actors I'd worked with, nobody quite had the presence of Ralph Fiennes. That's not to say that he was as scary as Voldemort himself - his face was always covered in green dots so that the visual effects people would be able to remove his nose (spoiler alert: he has a nose in real life). And I won't lie, it was funny seeing Voldemort sitting in his chair wearing his green robes, with a cup of tea in one hand and a newspaper in the other. But while we were filming, he had a weighty presence. He wasn't like us kids, governed by Carreras's whistle. He was not Jason, exuberantly telling anecdotes. He was not Robbie Coltrane, playing games and messing about, Hagrid-like, with the kids. He had an otherness that set him apart from everyone else on set.

I found myself at the receiving end of Ralph's idiosyncratic methods when we filmed the final scene of the Battle of Hogwarts. We spent weeks blocking without rolling a single camera, with everybody in full costume. I've never been on a single set for so long. It was such an important scene that they wanted to film it every which way possible, to give the eight films the climax they deserved. And so there were plenty of beats that didn't end up in the finished film - including a moment when Draco throws Harry his wand for the final duel with Voldemort. Just imagine! There's a roll of film somewhere showing Draco saving the day, but no one will ever see it. For me, though, the big moment was walking towards Voldemort at my father's insistence. I must have done that walk thirty or forty times. For many of the takes I did the same thing: walking past Voldemort, keeping my distance, pacing slowly, head down, slightly terrified. Ralph would look at me differently every time. Sometimes he'd smile. Sometimes he wouldn't. Sometimes he would break off his monologue and tell me to go back. It could be confusing - were we cutting, were we still filming? Occasionally he would repeat lines he'd previously delivered in the same take, each time in a very different way.

In the middle of one take, as I was pacing towards him for the umpteenth time, he lifted his arm just a fraction. It was the slightest movement, but enough to stop me in my tracks and think: is he trying to hug me? Uncertain, I shimmied towards him, my arms down by my side. He put his own arms around me and gave me perhaps the most uninviting hug ever captured on film. Even on set it chilled me. A hug from Voldemort was scary for Draco, and it was equally awkward for Tom. It gave me goosebumps then, and the memory gives me goosebumps now.

That was one take out of fifty. I had no idea they were going to use it until I saw the film for the first time at the premiere in London. The audience was completely silent. There was something so very twisted about that moment, something so wrong about watching Voldemort's warped display of affection, that I could sense everybody around me holding their breath uncomfortably. It was great! Then I went to the premiere in America. I sat there eagerly waiting for the same response. I watched myself approach the most evil dark wizard of all time. I saw him give me that super-awkward cuddle. I sat expectantly. I waited for the shocked silence. And then I heard everybody in the audience collapse into fits of laughter. The American audience found it absolutely hilarious. To this day I have no idea why. But I love it!

• • •

The late Helen McCrory, who played my mother, Narcissa Malfoy, joined us on the sixth film. There were originally discussions for her to play Bellatrix Lestrange, but she fell pregnant and decided not to take the part and to focus on being a mum. Some people might have found it intimidating, joining a tight-knit group of Malfoys and assorted Death Eaters, playing against the on-screen tension between Jason and Ralph. But I never got the impression that she felt intimidated for a moment. She was way too cool for that.

Helen was *effortlessly* cool. She would sit there quietly, rolling her own cigarettes with liquorice papers, and never feeling the need to talk over other people or speak just for the sake of speaking. She could look really quite stern, as though she could put you on the floor any time she wanted to, but I learned that she was soft-natured at heart. I soon found myself comfortable enough to ask her all sorts of questions about life, love and everything in between, and she was always free with her time and advice without ever talking down to me. Her approach was completely different to that of Jason or Ralph. When she slipped into character there was no sudden flick of the switch as there was with Jason, and no long, dramatic silences as there was with Ralph. Her transition was barely perceptible, but when she became Narcissa there was something in the eyes that told you everything you needed to know about her character: you could see the Malfoy coldness, but you could also see a softer side to her nature. I barely had to look at her and I found myself understanding something deeper about Draco.

We are never explicitly told why he feels so terrified about the prospect of killing Dumbledore, but here is my theory. If we were only able to see the influence of Draco's father, his reaction might not make sense. But we also see the influence of his mother, Narcissa, the woman who is prepared to lie to Voldemort to save her son. It is that influence that gives Draco his humanity, and if I managed to capture any of that in my performance in the sixth film, it was in part thanks to Helen's remarkable acting. In her own quiet way, she shaped what I was doing as much as anybody.

In the Voldemort-cuddle scene, when Draco is unsure whether to leave the Hogwarts students and join the Death Eaters, it's the urgency of his father's call that gets his attention. It's the softness of his mother that makes his decision. It was Helen's ability to render the softer side of Narcissa's personality that gave Draco the reason to walk. In art, as in life, I found it hard to say no to my mum.

24

ALL THINGS MUST PASS

or

THE GIRL FROM THE GREAT HALL

I'd like to take you back to the beginning of the book. It's my last day filming my first ever movie, *The Borrowers,* and I'm sitting in the make-up chair having my orange perm cut out. It suddenly hits me that the project is over. Sadness crashes over me and I start to cry. I blame it on the make-up lady, saying she poked me with her scissors, but that's not the truth at all. The truth is that I'm not good with things being over.

But all things must pass, as my favourite Beatle would say.

The final Potter movie was a colossal endeavour because it was two films shot together, as opposed to the usual six-month break between the previous films. The shoot seemingly went on forever. I wasn't there for even a quarter of the time that Daniel, Emma and Rupert were, so goodness knows how they felt about the marathon. The final days, however, came round a lot quicker than I would have hoped. We'd spent half our life thinking that the end was nowhere near in sight, but it crept up quickly on us all. At the same time there was a general sense of relief as the finishing post came into sight. But relief is not the same as happiness, and when my final day on set came, I knew what to expect of myself. I had form, after all.

My final day was a second-unit shoot. We filmed Draco leaving the battle, hurrying along a rubble-strewn bridge before he stops for a moment, turns, has a bit of a think, and then walks on. It was one of many scenes that didn't end up in the film. When the time came for us to wrap, I made a supreme effort to keep a lid on my emotions. I quickly shook the crew by the hand and muttered a few clipped British goodbyes. Then I left.

The moment I was in the car, I started to bawl. The tears wouldn't stop, but I did my best to hide them from Jimmy, my driver. This time round I had nobody to blame them on, so I just let them come. Whenever people ask me about that moment, they expect to hear about fond farewells with Daniel, Emma, Rupert and the rest of the cast. But none of them were present on my last day, and in any case, some of my very closest friends were part of the camera department, the special effects crew or the hair and make-up team. They'd been a huge part of my life for such a long time, and I felt as sad to be leaving them as I did to be leaving any of the actors. It was a melancholy thought, knowing that I would not be seeing many of those people so regularly, or even ever again, not out of choice but out of life moving on.

• • •

I'd had other acting experiences outside of Potter. Between the fifth and the sixth films, I took a part in a production called *The Disappeared*. It was a low-budget affair, which also starred Rupert Grint's partner Georgina, and was mostly shot in the underground caverns under London. As an experience it couldn't have been more different to the wizarding world.

From an acting point of view, it was more of a challenge. So much of Potter relied on the costumes and the sets. As long as you turned up and looked the part, that was half the job done. Here, I found myself having to dig a little deeper in my portrayal of a guy whose friend's brother is snatched, and who ends up having his neck broken by a maniac priest (my mum enjoyed that about as much as she enjoyed the spooky rubber Tom). And it was different in terms of scale. I was used to spending four hours blocking a scene, surrounded by a vast crew and all the paraphernalia of a high-budget movie set. Now I found myself on a council estate playground in Elephant and Castle in the middle of the night, with someone not much older than me holding the camera, with no rehearsal time because we were inevitably behind schedule from the moment we walked on set. For the first time I found myself around actors straight out of drama school rather than big stars, in a more improvisatory environment. On Potter the script was so tightly controlled that there was almost no scope for improvisation, no matter how hard Jason Isaacs tried to slip in extra lines. I was learning that on other projects dialogue and character development were up for discussion in a much more collaborative process. It was a huge learning curve for me.

For the first time, too, I was allowed to drive myself to set. I had to get there on my own and figure things out for myself. So while *The Disappeared* was undoubtedly important in widening my horizons as an actor, it was in some ways much more important in my development as a normal person.

Blending in always seemed better to me than being recognised. In that respect I was lucky. I'd managed to avoid making Harry Potter the most prominent part of my life. Lots of pursuits were more important to me: fishing, music, cars, hanging out with my friends. Potter was four or five places down on the list. I think it must have been much more difficult for Daniel, Emma and Rupert. Potter had been the primary focus of their lives, whereas for me acting in the Potter movies was just another thing that I did.

People might find this difficult to believe, but it's true. In fact, counterintuitively, the attention I've attracted because of my involvement with Potter has increased almost beyond recognition since the films have ended. Back then, I could quite easily walk along the street, even with luminous blond hair, without being recognised, without somebody shouting my name. Now it's harder. With each year that passes, Potter seems to become more popular. I find it hard to pinpoint why that should be the case. Ultimately, I think it must be because of the brilliance of the original stories. Unlike many of the children's stories written around the same time, the Harry Potter books and films are being passed down from one generation to the next. They are one of the few cultural landmarks that link thirteen-year-olds and thirty-year-olds. It means that there has been a snowball effect as more and more people get drawn into the wizarding world. If I had been told while we were making the films that in the years to come there would be a Harry Potter theme park, and that I'd be cutting the red ribbon on our own section of Universal Studios, I'd have laughed in your face.

So, although there was inevitably some sadness when the final film came to an end, I was also able to enjoy the relief. I could enjoy not having to sit in the make-up chair with my hair in foils every week. I could get back to concentrating solely on the ordinary part of my life. Even though I'd received encouragement from the likes of Michael Gambon, Alan Rickman and Jason Isaacs, I didn't find myself particularly focused on developing my acting career. I didn't hanker after great fame or outrageous success. I didn't really see the point of it. I was twenty-two years old and happy with my Muggle life. I was happy to be back on civvy street, with my friends, my dog and my girlfriend.

• • •

I'd first noticed her when I was seventeen, around the time of the fourth film, in the Great Hall. There were more than a hundred extras who we would see regularly on set, and on this day she was one of them: a Gryffindork, I'm sorry to say. There was a rule that if you were a student in the Great Hall, you weren't allowed to wear make-up. It was not a rule she honoured. She was about the same age as me, had glowing, tanned skin and long, jet-black eyelashes. She looked absolutely gorgeous. I know mine was not the only head she turned.

Later I learned she was an assistant to the stunt coordinator. She stood out for many reasons, but mostly for being such a tiny thing surrounded by these stocky, burly stuntmen. One day I was in the office of the second assistant directors. The gorgeous girl from the Great Hall was there with a call sheet, helping to organise the stunt schedule for the day, and we got talking. I asked her if she fancied a cup of tea and a cigarette and she said, 'Sure, why not?' So I brewed us a couple of mugs and we went downstairs to loiter outside Door 5 with our drinks and my packet of Benson and Hedges Gold. I smoked far too much in those days, more out of something to do with my hands than anything else. I offered her a cigarette, not knowing at the time that she didn't smoke. She accepted one. Her eyes crossed slightly as she looked at it, and I think she managed two puffs before coughing violently.

'You don't smoke, do you?' I said.

'Yes,' she said. 'It's just ... these are a little strong for me.'

We carried on chatting and, as we did so, members of the crew came in and out of Door 5. It was a busy place to stand. One of the chaps from the props department approached. I knew him well, and we often chatted, but excruciatingly I'd forgotten his name and it was far too late to ask. 'Alright, Tom?' he asked cheerfully.

'Hello, mate,' I replied. I gave him my most winning smile and we chatted. When he disappeared into Door 5, I turned to her and decided to fess up. 'Oh my days, I can't believe that!' I said.

'What?'

'We've been working together for years, I know his face, we chat about his family ... but I don't even know his name!'

She didn't smile. She barely reacted. She just gave me a cool look and said, 'You don't know my name either, do you?'

Panic. She was right. I froze for a moment. Then I did that clicking-your-fingers thing you do when you pretend something's on the tip of your tongue. She let me squirm for a moment - more than a moment - then put me out of my misery. 'I'm Jade,' she said.

• • •

That was Jade in a nutshell. Sharp, quick-witted and a straight-talker. She was someone who cut through bullshit immediately. We became pretty close, pretty quick. Jade was feisty. She had to hold her own with the stunt boys, who, without wanting to generalise too much, were the geezers of the set. She would sneak into my trailer when she had some free time for a cup of tea, and once had to put up with all the stunt boys rushing in and pretending to beat me up and trash the place, just to embarrass her. I almost surprised myself when one day I said to her: 'Are we boyfriend and girlfriend?' She smiled at me. I smiled back, wider.

For our first proper date we went to London Zoo. I turned up at her parents' house in a new shiny red BMW M6. Her dad - who I ended up knowing affectionately as Stevie G - had the same car, but the slightly tamer version. It looked the same, but there wasn't much under the bonnet. Mine was far flashier. Jade's dad opened the front door to see a bloke with white-blond hair and a car far too powerful for any nineteen-year-old, ready to take his only daughter out for a day in London. He'd have been quite within his rights to give me a stringent cross-examination, or at the very least a suspicious eyeballing. But, as I soon learned, he was far too kind-hearted for that, and he took my teenage flashness in his stride and reserved judgement. Anyone else at the time would have thought I looked a right twat. Looking back, even I think I must have looked like a right twat. Jade and I held hands for the first time at London Zoo and smoked a couple of more tolerable menthol cigarettes, and even though my luminous hair was the full Draco, nobody stopped us or even seemed to notice us. Or more likely we just didn't notice anyone else.

From there, things moved quickly. A few months later I took her to Venice for her nineteenth birthday (miraculously Stevie G rubber-stamped the idea). Poor decision, Tom. The smart move would have been to start lower and move up. Once you've booked into a ridiculously fancy hotel in the most romantic city in the world, it doesn't leave much room for improvement. But I guess I was trying to impress her. We went to Harry's Bar, one of the swankiest restaurants in the world, two kids surrounded by rich adults. After one Bellini too many, the waiter had to politely ask me to keep my voice down. We had a lot of fun.

Years later, when Harry Potter finished, and I'd got all my crying out of the way, we went on holiday to Italy again to celebrate our time on the films. I'd shaved off my blond hair and we were quietly celebrating the end of the Potter marathon together. I had no real plans for the future. I certainly didn't really expect to be back on a film set any time soon. So when my agent called me in Italy to say I'd been offered a part in a major movie, I was taken aback. The movie was called *Rise of the Planet of the Apes* and it meant getting on a plane the following week and flying to Vancouver.

To this day, I don't know how or why they plucked me out of so many people who could have played the role. I was acutely aware, even at the time, that my ten years of work on Harry Potter was largely down to the fact that I'd turned up one day for an audition when I was twelve. If I hadn't done so, another person would have performed the part just as successfully. This was different. A massive Hollywood movie starring James Franco and Andy Serkis, with a budget of hundreds of millions of dollars, for which the filmmakers could pretty much take their pick of any actors in the world. And they'd chosen me without even asking me to audition? It was baffling, but I couldn't help finding it very cool. It was a moment when I first considered my future as an actor and it looked kind of rosy.

Rise of the Planet of the Apes was the first project I'd been involved with that got my dad excited. He was a fan of the Charlton Heston original, which I had never seen. I didn't even know at the time that one of my lines was infamous: 'Take your stinking paws off me, you damn dirty ape!' All I knew was that it sounded like a brand new adventure, and I gratefully accepted the offer.

Harry Potter had been substantial as film productions go, of course, but there was still something humble and British about tawdry old Leavesden Studios, about grabbing a breath of fresh air outside Door 5. On a major Hollywood movie, everything is bigger and better. Take, for example, the catering. I found myself on set in Vancouver being asked if I wanted something from the 'crafty'.

'What's that?' I said.

'Craft services,' they said.

'What's that?' I repeated.

I was led to a massive food truck that would serve me *whatever* I wanted, *whenever* I wanted it. Cookies, toasties, crisps, you name it. You want ice cream at two o'clock in the morning? No problem. What flavour? Think my doppelgänger Macaulay Culkin ordering room service in *Home Alone 2*.

And this, it seemed, was going to be my life. A life of free ice cream in the small hours. A life where, with only the formality of a phone call from my agent, I would be whisked from one major film set to another. I thought, *This is it. This is what the future's going to be.*

Turned out I was wrong.

25

BEYOND THE WAND

or

LONELY IN LA-LA LAND

R*ise of the Planet of the Apes* was a one-off. It was the first time I'd ever been offered a major part without auditioning for it, and it wouldn't happen again for a long while. A lucky break that wasn't to be repeated any time soon.

If I'd been left to my own devices, it might well have been my last film. I lacked the drive to assert myself and fulfil the potential that, according to Jason and others, I'd shown towards the end of the Potter project. I even found myself wondering if I wouldn't be happier ditching the acting to become a professional angler. Jade, thankfully, had other ideas for me. Had it not been for her encouragement, I wouldn't have a career now. When it became clear that I would have to throw myself back into the world of auditioning, we set up a mobile camera rig (this was pre-iPhone, people) and wherever we were she would read with me - crucial, because without someone to read with, you're hitting a tennis ball up against the wall. At her instigation, we recorded countless self-tapes, for which the strike rate was about one in a hundred. In the meantime, an old schoolfriend managed to blag me a part in a miniseries filming in Cape Town called *Labyrinth*, a historical fantasy with John Hurt and Sebastian Stan.

My part was that of Viscount Trencavel. The character couldn't have been more different to Draco Malfoy. It required a Braveheart-esque wig (fortunately I was no stranger to weird hairdos) and a suit of chainmail and, as part of the performance, a grand entrance into his castle to deliver a heroic speech in front of a vast crowd. In fact, there were two heroic speeches in this film and the prospect of both terrified me. I knew Draco so well. Throw me into any kind of scenario and I knew how he would react. To create something from the ground up, without meeting any of the cast or crew in advance, was daunting. And while I was used to productions of a certain scale, I was no longer in my comfort zone of Leavesden Studios, of my trailer and Door 5. When I turned up on set I gave myself a good talking-to. You've got this, Tom. Just relax. I met the director for the first time on set that morning and a couple of hours later I was striding through a crowd of chain-mailed background artists ready to deliver my first monologue.

Here's the thing about background artists: some of them are into it and some of them are not. Some maintain their focus, others struggle to hide their boredom. So when I stood in front of them on my first take, ready to say my piece and slightly bricking it, I saw, looking back at me, a sea of focused faces, except one. This face stood out: a teenager, younger than the rest of them, with an expression that reminded me of myself back in the day. He looked at me with total, Draco-like disdain, just as I would have done. I could almost hear his thoughts: *Oh yeah? Matey in his little wig is going to go up there and belt out a bunch of thees and thous? What a nobhead!*

He didn't know it, but he'd tapped into all the insecurities I was feeling. And so I made a decision on the spot: I was going to deliver my monologue directly to him. Instead of my eyes darting around the rest of the crowd, I was laser-focused on him. And I was going to take a leaf out of the Ralph Fiennes playbook and let silence do my talking for me. I stared at him. I let the awkwardness build. I saw him look from left to right, clearly wondering: is he looking at me? Gradually, I could sense that he, and the rest of the cast, were taking me seriously. And so, drawing a bit of confidence from the moment, I delivered my rousing speech the best I knew how. Whether it was any good or not is for other people to say, but with the benefit of hindsight I thank that cocky young extra. He gave me the rocket fuel I needed, and the impetus to put into action the lessons I'd learned over the years from many older actors about how to keep someone's attention.

My second rousing monologue was a little less successful. Before offering me the part, the producer had gone through the standard procedure of checking various logistics with me on the phone. Are you available on these dates? Is your passport current? Do you have a driving licence? You learn, as an actor, that the correct answer to all these pre-shoot questions is: yes. Can you speak Swahili? Fluently! Can you manage a French accent? Mais oui, monsieur! So when the producer asked if I knew how to ride a horse, I naturally gave them the answer they wanted to hear. Mate, I was practically born in the saddle!

It wasn't a total lie. Growing up, our neighbour kept horses and as a little kid I would occasionally be placidly led around on horseback. But I was actually quite scared of horses, and those childhood rides were very different to what was expected of me on this occasion. I was to ride up and down a line of a hundred knights, all in chainmail and holding swords and shields, as I declaimed heroically. At the climax of my speech, I was to dig my heels into the stallion's flanks and gallop off, leading my army into battle.

The horse had other ideas. On my first take, as I reached the critical moment, shouting my war cry, sword aloft, about to lead my mighty army to glory, I urged him on with my heels in heroic fashion. The extras roared, ready to follow their fearless leader to death or glory. The horse, however, found my speech less inspirational. He showed about as much interest in galloping into battle as that teenage extra had shown on my first day on set. So we tried it again. 'For honour! For family! For freedom!' For fuck's sake ... the horse could barely bring itself to trot. I saw the director and producer behind the monitor shaking their heads. This clearly looked ridiculous. We needed a solution.

The horse trainer on set was a petite lady and my character sported an enormous Snape-like cloak. The trainer sat behind me on the horse, covered by my curiously bulging cloak, holding on to my waist. The horse had rather more respect for her than it did for me. When the moment came, she gently nudged the animal's flanks and my mighty steed bolted furiously. It was absolutely terrifying. I desperately gripped the reins and, wide-eyed and white-faced, did everything I could not to fall off as it galloped into battle. My expression, when I saw it played back, was one of abject terror. I wasn't surprised when that moment didn't make the final cut.

That was not my last unfortunate horse moment. In 2016 Kevin Reynolds, who had previously directed *Robin Hood: Prince of Thieves* and was one of my favourite directors, asked me to be part of his biblical drama *Risen*. I was to play a Roman soldier alongside Joseph Fiennes, Ralph's brother, who massively took me under his wing. An early pivotal scene involved us riding on horseback, through another huge crowd of extras, all pelting us with papier mâché rocks, to the crucifixion. Here, Joseph's character was to have a conversation with Jesus, while I sat quietly on horseback to one side.

The horses had been rehearsing this scene for hours without us. But they didn't know that the rocks were made of papier mâché, and were understandably skittish. What my horse most definitely knew, however, was that the plank on its back - me - was no jockey. As Joseph Fiennes delivered his fantastic performance, my steed refused to stand still. It rotated one way then the other, into the crowd then out of it. I was completely incapable of controlling the bloody thing. I heard Kevin shout: 'Cut! What the *hell* is going on?' I gave a feeble apology and in the end we had to dress up one of the horse trainers in the garb of a Roman soldier so that he could hold the horse still while I sat sheepishly in the saddle.

That was the last time I tried to ride a horse on camera.

• • •

As a kid, I'd auditioned for a hundred different projects before Potter came along. I'd grown quite used to being told no back then. Now I was going to have to get used to it again. I found myself auditioning every couple of weeks, and being rejected almost as frequently. I was aware, of course, that some people were surprised that I had to audition, but in truth it didn't really cross my mind that I would be offered anything. It wasn't like I had a diverse showreel. It seemed crazy to me, now that I was faced with the prospect of developing a career as an actor, that I should have been handed *Rise of the Planet of the Apes* without anybody so much as checking my American accent. It felt more normal to be at the sharp end of the jobbing actor's life.

Again, had it been left up to me, I might have remained in that state of limbo. But Jade was a driving force, and Alan Radcliffe had given me good advice: find yourself a good agent, go to LA and put yourself in as many rooms as possible. And so I did just that.

Someone once said that New York has four times as much work for an actor as London, and LA has four times as much work as New York. Do the maths and it's easy to understand why so many thousands of actors from across the world find their way to Hollywood. It's a town of contradictions: full of success and failure, wealth and poverty - it's exciting and daunting in equal measure. I saw, in those early days, every side of LA. I would shack up in a nondescript Hollywood hotel for a couple of weeks at a time, try to read three scripts a day and have some face time with as many players as possible.

Some doors were open to me. An LA agency accepted me as their client. They took me to lunch at the Beverly Wilshire Hotel and took great pride in telling me that this was where the film *Pretty Woman* had been filmed. I nodded politely but didn't tell them I'd never seen *Pretty Woman*. I felt out of place, a kid from Surrey being wined and dined at one of Hollywood's most exclusive and fashionable spots. Between you and me, I'd have preferred a box of chicken nuggets. Back in their office I found myself in front of six people looking at me with the eager light of enthusiasm shining in their eyes, telling me that I was going to be a Big Star and they knew exactly how to get me there. Every couple of minutes a new face would walk in, shake me by the hand and tell me what a huge fan they were, and how exciting it was that I might become part of their team. I thought, *Great! Bit weird but I could get used to this.*

Other doors were harder to penetrate. My first audition in LA was for the part of a teacher in a TV pilot. I didn't realise it at the time, but they make thousands of TV pilots in Hollywood, for various series, most of which are never eventually commissioned. They are the disposable napkins of the film industry. I didn't understand this. For me, everything was potentially another Harry Potter. So when I turned up at the studio for the audition, I was unprepared for what awaited me. It didn't matter that a huge Harry Potter poster hung behind the security desk, I still had difficulty explaining who I was, why I was there and gaining access to the studio. Once I made it to the audition room it became clear that I was one of countless hopefuls. I was given a place to sit with at least a dozen others and waited for three or four people to audition before me. I could hear everything that was going on in the audition room - not the norm in the UK - and that did nothing for my nerves. My turn came. I walked into the audition room to see six people sitting in a line, looking bored and unimpressed. If they recognised me, they sure as hell didn't show it. I gave them my brightest smile and said: 'Hi! I'm Tom from England!'

They said nothing. I went down the line, shaking hands with them all, but when I got to number three or four, I started to suspect that this really wasn't a shaky-hand moment. One of them confirmed my suspicion by saying: 'Could you just go and stand on the X and say your lines?'

I looked over my shoulder and saw a gaffer-tape X on the floor. 'Right,' I said. 'Sorry.' And I took my place. As I stood there, they barely seemed to register that I was in the room. The reality of the situation clicked in my head. They'd been sitting here for hours. They'd heard this scene every which way it was possible to say it. It was for an unimportant character and they either didn't know or didn't care what I'd been in previously. On the contrary, they couldn't wait to get rid of me.

As these pennies dropped, my nerves went off the scale. The part for which I was auditioning was a nervous character, but I'm not sure that helped. I bumbled my way through my lines in a highly perplexing American accent - one line from Texas, one line from New Orleans, the next from Brooklyn - occasionally repeating myself to ensure that I'd said my words right. I was cringing and they were cringing more. Halfway through, three of them were on their phones. Never a good sign.

It was my first disastrous audition in LA. It wouldn't be my last (apologies once again, Sir Anthony ...). I'd like to say it gets easier. Truthfully, it doesn't. But I developed a strange kind of addiction to the process. Before each audition, I would stand outside the room and my nervous brain would try to enumerate all the reasons why I really didn't have to be there, why I should just walk away. But afterwards, the relief of having done it was like nothing else. No matter how good or bad the audition was, the ecstatic adrenaline rush gave me a unique buzz. I might be back at square one of the acting world, but I was getting a kick out of it.

LA can be a lonely place, especially at first. There are few experiences more confusing than being in that crazy city by yourself, trying to figure everything out. Each time I went back, however, I found that I knew a few more people. The more people I knew, the friendlier the place became. The friendlier it became, the more I was seduced by the weather, the upbeat attitudes and the quality of life. Despite its quirks, or maybe because of them, LA started to call to me. Jade and I had several brief stints living there, and when the opportunity arose to audition for a new TV series created by Stephen Bochco and to be shot in LA called *Murder in the First*, I went for it. We made countless self-tapes in Jade's parents' living room in London (thanks, Stevie G) and I went through endless rounds to land the part. Eventually, though, they told me I'd got it, so Jade and I moved out to LA with my dog, Timber.

And life was good. Everything was bigger, brighter and better. We found a tiny wooden bungalow in West Hollywood, painted white with a small garden and a picket fence. Gradually, as my work started to pick up, the excruciating loneliness of LA receded and the pleasures of being a person in the public eye in that city started to show themselves. In England, nobody cared if you were famous. If they did care, they usually pointed and muttered to their friend, or at best they'd come over and ask: ''Ere, you that wizard geezer? You know, the one from that thing?' Plus a sarcastic comment, more often than not. In LA, as my face and name started to become better known, the initial coolness faded away and suddenly it seemed that almost *everybody* cared that I was famous, in a way that massaged my ego like never before. Effusive strangers claimed to *love* my work. My *work*? As far as I could tell, I'd never done a real day's work in my life, other than back at the fishery car park in Surrey. But who was I to argue, especially when people started treating me like a bona-fide film star? I'd never experienced that before. Growing up I'd thankfully been kept firmly in my place by three older brothers. At school and beyond, I was never allowed to feel different. Now, everybody in LA started treating me like somebody I wasn't.

It started with clothes. People would give me designer clothes. For nothing? For nothing. Awesome. It moved on to cars. I met somebody who looked after BMW's VIP fleet. Never in my life had I considered myself to be a VIP, whatever that even meant. Suddenly I was one, apparently, and they'd lend me different cars seemingly whenever I wanted them. We'd turn up at a club with a queue of people outside because it was *the* place to be seen, and the red velvet rope would be lifted immediately and we'd be ushered in without having to wait, because that's what happens when you're a 'movie star'. My world became one of crazy opportunity, elaborate nights out and - there's no other way of putting it - cool free shit. I enjoyed it. Jade enjoyed it.

I mean, who wouldn't?

• • •

If you tell a person he's great enough times, he'll start to believe it. If you blow enough smoke up someone's arse, sooner or later they'll start breathing it in. It's almost inevitable. I'd turn up outside some new fancy restaurant in a bright orange Lamborghini I'd been given for the week, and waiters would scurry to lead me to an exclusive table I'd only managed to reserve at the very last minute because of my name, while paparazzi took pictures of my incredibly subtle entrance. The old Tom would have been straight on the blower to his brother to tell him how mental it was. He would have been constantly kicking himself, because this was *insane*! The new Tom didn't do that. The new Tom pretended it was normal. Of course you've saved me a table at this exclusive restaurant with a waiting list as long as the Golden Gate Bridge. Of *course* you have.

I acted the way I was treated. For a while it was lots of fun. But only for a while. The gleam soon began to tarnish.

I never knew I wanted this kind of life. And as time passed, an uncomfortable truth quietly presented itself to me: I *didn't* want it. Perhaps it sounds ungrateful. I don't mean it to. I was in a lucky and privileged position. But there was something inauthentic about the life I was leading. I realised that, more often than not, I didn't *want* to go to this premiere, or that fancy restaurant, or whatever Caribbean island we had earmarked for our next getaway. I missed my old life. I missed fishing by the lake with Chris. I missed watching *Beavis and Butt-Head* with Ash. I missed making music with Jink. I missed smoking a crafty spliff with my friends on a park bench. I missed those days where my spare time could be spent with a beat to rap over, rather than being peddled out on the celebrity circuit. I missed having an ordinary conversation with an authentic human, who didn't know who I was, and didn't care. I missed my mum.

I should have noticed these feelings and made a change. I should have voiced my worries, if to no one else, at least to myself. It was up to me, after all. But something strange had started to happen. Placed into an environment where people were desperate to do things for me, I started to lose the ability to do things, and think things, for myself. Having allowed my newly appointed LA team to encourage me with my acting career and expose me to this new Hollywood lifestyle, I felt like I had gone a step further and outsourced my ability to make any kind of decision, or have an opinion of my own. If people remind you often enough how lucky you are, and that a certain way of living is cool, you start to believe it even if you don't feel it deep down. Suddenly your critical faculties are turned to jelly and you stop being your own person. Bit by bit, I wasn't myself anymore.

The more immersed I became in the smoke and mirrors of Hollywood, the less chance I had to meet people who didn't know who I was and, more to the point, didn't care. Daily I found myself having less genuine human interaction with people. There always seemed to be an undercurrent. A subtext. An agenda. I wasn't being myself. For as long as I could remember, I'd mimicked my dad's self-deprecating buffoonery. That sense of humour was second nature to me, an integral part of who I was. But in the company I was keeping in LA, it didn't translate. Everyone took themselves too seriously. Everyone took *me* too seriously.

And maybe, beneath the surface, there were other matters at play. My family were not strangers to mental health issues. Ash had been hospitalised as a boy, Jink as an adult. A predisposition to such problems was in my blood. It's easy for me to paint a portrait of a young man corrupted by Hollywood, but perhaps there was more to it than that. There's no doubt that LA made me feel peculiarly lonely and disassociated from myself: feelings, surely, that could trigger mental health difficulties in anybody. Perhaps these difficulties are more easily camouflaged when you're sitting beyond the velvet ropes or behind the wheel of the shiny orange Lamborghini.

I craved an escape from the version of myself I was becoming. I craved human contact with people who cared nothing for the red carpet lifestyle. I craved the old me. I craved authenticity.

I found it in a bar called Barney's Beanery.

26

THE BALLAD OF BARNEY'S BEANERY

or

IF I WERE A RICH MAN

Let me tell you about Barney's Beanery.

Nothing's old in Los Angeles, but as far as pubs go, Barney's is one of the oldest. It's a dive bar that bears the battle scars of the past sixty years. There's a plaque dedicating a seat to Jim Morrison of the Doors where he used to sit, and the walls are plastered with memorabilia from every decade from the sixties onwards. The memorabilia records the passing of time like rings on a tree trunk. Maybe that's why I liked it. Barney's has seen it all. It doesn't care who you are.

And nor do the people who frequent it: a colourful mixture of don't-give-a-fudgers, as far removed from the beautiful people of the Hollywood circuit that you could wish to meet. These were my people. I didn't have to pretend in front of them. I could be the easy-going joker my dad had taught me to be.

During my mid-to-late twenties I spent more hours, more nights, than I care to remember at Barney's. Before that, I wasn't much of a drinker. A glass of champagne at a wedding, maybe, but not much more than that. But when you spend a lot of time in dive bars craving normality, it inevitably leads to a lot of drinking. I went from being not particularly interested to regularly having a few pints a day before the sun had even gone down, and a shot of whiskey to go with each of them.

Drinking becomes a habit at the best of times. When you're drinking to escape a situation, even more so. The habit spilled out of the bar and, from time to time, on to set. It came to the point where I would think nothing of having a drink while I was working. I'd turn up unprepared, not the professional I wanted to be. The alcohol, though, wasn't the problem. It was the symptom. The problem was deeper and it drew me, almost nightly, to Barney's. I'd sit at the bar, a beer constantly in front of me, maybe something stronger, and I'd shoot the shit with the regulars. Well into the small hours, I'd while away the time drinking, talking nonsense, playing shuffleboard. I told myself I was having a good time there, and on some level I was. On another level, though, I was hiding from something. Myself, perhaps, or the situation I found myself in. And Barney's was a good place to hide.

I struck up friendships with the bartenders - female, mostly. These girls had seen it all, were hard as nails and were not known for their friendliness. After about six months they softened slightly towards me and we started having a laugh. They had wicked senses of humour. For me, half the attraction of a night at Barney's was the prospect of us hanging out and taking the piss out of each other. And that's what I did, the night before my life changed for ever.

I should have been tucked up in bed that evening, because the following day I had what I expected to be an important meeting at the office of my managers. It had only been in the diary for twenty-four hours, but I knew that it was potentially a big deal. In the normal course of events, if a member of my team had a script that they wanted me to consider, they'd send it over for me to read before we discussed it. On this occasion, though, I was being asked by my manager to go into the office to talk about something unseen that I didn't need to read beforehand. I naturally assumed it meant a big project was on the table. I was pumped.

Far from being tucked up in bed, however, I'd spent all night at Barney's. I'd had zero sleep and was a little the worse for wear, having had perhaps seven whiskeys too many. I said goodnight to the girls and that I'd see them tomorrow. As I valet-parked the Beamer outside my management's office block the next morning, I felt pretty chipper, especially with the prospect of a big offer on the table. The office was housed in a glass skyscraper in one of the swankier parts of Los Angeles. I took the long elevator ride to the top, still tipsy from the night before, and signed in at reception. A couple of minutes later, my manager arrived to show me in to the meeting.

Did I detect a slight curtness in his demeanour, a slight restraint? I think perhaps I did, but I was looking forward to hearing what this was all about, so I paid it no real attention.

You wouldn't know to look at it, but the building itself had been a bank in the past. There weren't any Gringotts-like counting tables, heavy ledgers or dusty clerks. It was sleek and modern. But there was a big old circular bank-vault door, which led to an office where all the especially important meetings were held. I felt a bit of a tingle as my manager led me towards it. We were in the vault! Alright! This has to be good news!

We crossed the threshold into the office. My blood turned to ice.

It wasn't a huge room. Big enough for one meeting table, me, and the seven other people sitting silently in a circle, waiting. Jade was there, sitting next to two of my agents. My lawyer. Both of my managers. And one big, bald, scary stranger.

Nobody spoke. They stared at me. I knew immediately that I'd been brought here under false pretences. I knew that this was nothing to do with some spectacular, career-defining acting job. Quite what they wanted with me, I *didn't* know. But the look in their eyes and the energy in the room told me it wasn't good. I'd heard of interventions, when friends and family congregate to tell a person that they're in serious, life-threatening trouble. But I *wasn't* in serious trouble. Was I? This couldn't be that.

Could it?

I crumbled to the floor like a soggy towel. The room seemed to spin. I found myself shaking my head and muttering to myself: 'I can't do this. I can't *do* this ...' Nobody spoke. They just continued to look at me in that bleak, serious way. I staggered out of the room, my pulse thumping. They let me go. I went outside to try to calm myself with a cigarette, escorted by the big, bald stranger, but calm was not an emotion I was capable of at that moment. A crushing, relentless sense of betrayal and violation burned inside me. Everyone in my professional life and - worse than that - the person closest to me had conspired to get me here. I hadn't seen it coming at all. I was angry. I was tired. Truth to tell, I was very hungover. I gave some thought to simply running away. But for some reason I didn't. I went back into the building and through the vault door. Everybody was still there. Still staring at me, in a way that chilled and infuriated me. I sat down, unwilling - unable - to meet anybody's gaze. And then the big bald guy, the one person in the room I didn't recognise, took charge.

He was a professional interventionist. The guy they call when they want to be certain about the outcome of an intervention. My management company had paid for him to manage the process. It's not a service that comes cheap and he was good at his job. There was nothing he hadn't seen. No reaction I could have displayed that he hadn't predicted. He explained that right now he knew I would be feeling angry but at some point I would manage to forgive the people in the room for what they'd done. I told him to fuck off with my eyes. Forgiveness didn't seem at all likely to me. I was exhausted. I was spinning. I was hanging. The night before I'd been in Barney's talking openly and honestly to my acquaintances there. Now I was surrounded by so-called friends who had lied to me, who had tricked me into thinking I had a new job in order to ensnare me here. They were dissemblers. I couldn't understand why, if they were so worried, they couldn't have just come to my house and talked to me in the usual way? Forgiveness? Fuck that. I was a long way from forgiveness.

Everybody in the room had written me a letter. They read them out, one after the other. The letters were generally fairly brief. Most of them I seem to have excised from my memory. I listened to Jade and the others as they told me how concerned they were about my behaviour, about my drinking and my substance abuse. I was in no state to hear them. As far as I was concerned, my vices amounted to no more than a few beers a day, the odd whiskey and maybe a couple of spliffs. It wasn't like I was waking up with an empty bottle of vodka in my hand, surrounded by a pool of my own vomit. I wasn't hiding out in crack dens, smoking opium, or unable to work, or out of control. When Jade spoke, I remember thinking: did you instigate this just because you think I've been less than the perfect boyfriend? She hadn't, of course. In fact, she'd only found out about the intervention hours before. But my anger and frustration put thoughts in my head that shouldn't have been there.

One letter, though, hit the hardest. It was written by the person in the room who I knew the least. My lawyer, whom I'd barely ever met face to face, spoke with quiet honesty. 'Tom,' he said, 'I don't know you very well, but you seem like a nice guy. All I want to tell you is that this is the seventeenth intervention I've been to in my career. Eleven of them are now dead. Don't be the twelfth.'

His were the words that cut through my anger and denial. And even though I still saw this as a massive overreaction to a non-existent problem, his stark plea made me bow my head.

We'd been at this for two hours by now. Everybody had said what they wanted to say. Everyone was drained. Nobody more so than me.

'What do you want me to do?' I pleaded.

'We want you to go into treatment,' the interventionist said.

'Rehab?'

'Rehab.'

One thing you should know about Californian rehabilitation clinics: they're expensive. Some can charge upwards of

$40,000 a month. Forty grand to stay in a rehab centre against my will? You must be fucking joking. The very notion was absurd. But the intervention had shocked me. The pressure to do what I was told was immense. 'Fine,' I petulantly told them. 'I'll go to your little rehab clinic if it's so important to you. I'll not drink for thirty days, if you really believe it's such a problem.'

Silence.

The interventionist said: 'We have a place booked in Malibu and we want you to go now.'

'Fine,' I said. 'I'll go home and sort my shit out. I can fit it in tomorrow, maybe the day after.'

He shook his head. 'No. We have a car waiting. We want you to go *now*. Straight there. No detours.'

I blinked. Were they insane? This was preposterous. Was I so far gone that this couldn't wait twenty-four hours? What had people been telling them? How the hell did we land here? Did I have any say in this at all?

I was told, quite clearly, that no, I didn't have a choice. 'If you don't get help now,' one of my managers said, 'we won't be able to represent you anymore.' End of.

'I need my guitar,' I said.

They told me no.

'I need a change of clothes.'

They told me no.

My protests continued for another hour. Everybody was immovable. I was to get in the car with the interventionist, and I had to do it now.

And so, finally, I gave in. I was all out of fight.

It was one of the more surreal moments of my life, relinquishing all command and walking out of that shiny glass office building in the company of the interventionist, to his vehicle. The journey to Malibu took about an hour. A long, solemn hour as we sat side by side in silence. As Malibu approached, he turned to me and said, 'You want to stop and get a final beer? Before we check you in?'

I guess he was just trying to make things easier for me, but at the time I couldn't fathom his question. Everyone had just told me I had a problem with substances. I didn't agree with them, not at the time, but why would I stop for a beer and make it look as if they were right all along? 'No, I don't want to stop for a fucking beer,' I told him.

He nodded. 'Okay then,' he said. We fell into silence again as the miles passed while I chain-smoked cigarettes – the one vice they didn't have a problem with. And before long the gates of the rehab centre came into view.

• • •

The centre was situated on the floor of a vast canyon, a mile and a half down a zig-zag road, surrounded by the thick forests of Malibu. As we trundled down that road, a kind of numbness fell over me. It was a beautiful location. Breathtaking, really. But I would rather have been anywhere else but there.

The interventionist dropped me off outside a big white house at the bottom of the canyon. It was a nice-looking place, and for $40,000, so it should have been. I'd barely spoken in hours. As I crossed the threshold of the rehab centre, I felt as though I was in some kind of terrible dream. I checked in. They were expecting me and the big bald man left me in their care.

A nurse sat me down and asked me some questions. What substances are you using? And how much? How often? I answered honestly, but I was still of the view that I was the wrong person in the wrong place. I wasn't the kind of guy who needed a shot first thing in the morning just to get through the day. I wasn't doing a bit of smack on the side. This was all a big mistake. The nurse recorded my answers. Then she said: 'Would you like an alias?'

I didn't understand. 'What do you mean?' I asked.

'While you're here, you have to wear a name badge. If you'd prefer, we can use an alias. Like Bob, or Sam.'

I twigged. She'd recognised me, and I suppose she was trying to be sensitive to my situation. I was in no mood, though, to be handled. 'If people recognise me from the Harry Potter films,' I said, 'it'll be because of my face. It won't be because of what's written on my name tag. You could write "Mickey Fucking Mouse" on my chest and they're not going to think I'm him.'

Not unreasonably, the nurse became defensive. 'We just thought it would be a good way of protecting your anonymity,' she said.

For some reason the suggestion had made me irrationally angry. I took a deep breath to control my emotions. 'I don't want a fucking alias,' I said. The subject was quietly dropped.

Next, I had to endure a two-hour medical induction. They took blood samples and urine samples. They checked my blood pressure. They made me blow into a Breathalyser. They shone torches into my eyes and prodded and poked me. And then they put me into detox.

Detox is the process of ensuring there are no substances in your system before you go into treatment. I still had some alcohol in my blood from the previous night, so they led me to a small room, very plain and white with dusty, bland furniture. This was definitely not the Beverly Wilshire Hotel. There were two beds and I shared the room with one other guy. He'd been there for three days and still wasn't blowing sober. I was scared. I had no idea who this man was. He was shaking on his bed, coming down from a meth bender, and mumbling incoherently. I felt sick, and stunned. I'd had a few too many whiskeys one night, and suddenly I was sharing a room with a meth-head. We talked a little. I didn't understand most of what he said but it was instantly apparent that he was suffering a lot worse than me. It didn't do much for my belief that I really shouldn't be there.

They'd given me some kind of sedative medication, so I slept deeply that night. When I woke up, they breathalysed me again and the test was negative. I'd been in detox for all of twelve hours before they let me out again. They gave me a tour of the facilities: the kitchen, the day room, the grounds. There was a ping-pong table. It reminded me that I was a long way from the recreation tent at the Potter studios, where Emma had good-naturedly slapped me in the face. That thought was a corkscrew in my gut. I thought of Emma a lot as I wondered how the hell I'd ended up here.

And of course they introduced me to some of the patients, who all sported name tags as if we were speed-dating. I quickly learned that the standard opening gambit in a place like this was: 'What's your DOC?' Your drug of choice. When people asked me that, I said weed and alcohol. After being asked, I felt obliged to return the question. The vast majority were in for what seemed to me to be much more serious predilections than mine: heroin, opioids, benzos, crystal meth, crack cocaine. Most drank, too, but that was secondary to their DOCs.

I don't want to give the impression that this was like *One Flew Over the Cuckoo's Nest*. Nobody was throwing faeces across the room, or screaming, or showing fits of rage. However, the side-effects of these people's addictions were extreme and startling. Most of them trembled uncontrollably and couldn't look you in the eye for more than a second. They tripped over their words. It was unsettling to say the least.

It was not only the patients who seemed alien to me. The whole concept of being in an American rehab centre was entirely foreign to a British kid from Surrey. The notion of paying ludicrous sums of money to segregate myself from the rest of humanity was discomfiting and frankly bizarre. I was the youngest person there, but the clientele weren't exactly old. I presumed that most of them had wealthy families who could fund their rehabilitation. Their upbringings, I felt, were a million miles from my own. These were not my people. This was not where I belonged. The sick feeling in my gut grew stronger.

The emotional drain of the past twenty-four hours was huge. That, and the medication they put me on to keep me steady, put me into a solemn, reclusive, almost passive state of mind. I somehow made it through the day, occasionally exchanging a few words with the other patients, but mostly keeping to myself. If anybody recognised me, they didn't show it. I guess their own problems preoccupied them fully. Why would they be interested in some Broomstick Prick from a wizard movie while they were going through their own personal hell?

Evening came. I ate dinner. I watched the sun setting high above me over the canyon ridge. I stepped outside into the grounds for a breath of fresh air. All I had on me was that dwindling packet of cigarettes. I had to ask somebody for a light. They'd told me earlier that if I wanted to smoke, I should sit on a designated bench but I ignored that instruction and instead sat on the grass. Nobody scolded me or asked me to move, so I just sat there with my cigarette, contemplating my situation and the events of the past couple of days. Clearly I'd reached a turning point in my life. I might not have agreed with the decisions of others that led to me being here. I definitely didn't think this was the right place for me. But here I was, and I had decisions to make. Was I going to engage with this rehabilitation centre?

Or was I going to take a different path?

I had no idea, as I sat there finishing my cigarette, that the next few hours would define the rest of my life. No clue that I would reach a terrible nadir, and that I would have to rely on the kindness of strangers to see me through. All I knew was that I was angry and that I didn't want to be here anymore.

So I stood up, and I began to walk.

• • •

I didn't really think, as I strode up the zig-zag road away from the rehab centre, that anything would come of my moment of rebellion. After I'd walked a couple of hundred metres, I remember thinking that any minute now one of the security people would sprint towards me and rugby tackle me to the ground. I'd be dragged back to my room, and that would be that.

But nobody sprinted. There were no rugby tackles.

Two minutes became five and five minutes became ten. The rehab centre disappeared from sight behind me. I continued walking up the steep zig-zag road, but even then I was convinced that I'd be rumbled. There would be security gates and cameras up ahead. There would be people on watch. Any second now they'll come and get me. I think I almost wanted to be caught. It would give me something else to be angry about.

But nobody appeared. I kept walking, and walking. A mile up the hill. Two miles. I reached the top and there was a fence. I managed to clamber over it. The terrain was a little treacherous underfoot. I was wearing my regular clobber and had nothing on me but a few cigarettes. No phone, no wallet, no money, no lighter. But I kept walking and before long I saw the lights of moving vehicles up ahead: the Pacific Coast Highway. I knew that the ocean lay beyond the PCH, and I've always had an affinity with the ocean. It called to me and I started to move in that direction.

I had it in my head that they'd be out searching for me by now. I switched into what I can only describe as *Grand Theft Auto* mode. Every time I saw a car approach, I ducked or dived into a bush or ditch, scratching my face and arms to ribbons. I hopped fences and ran through the shadows until I eventually reached a wild, deserted beach. The moon shone bright and by now I was covered in mud, blood and sweat. The urge took me to wade into the water. All of a sudden, the frustration burst out of me. I was, I realise now, completely sober for the first time in ages, and I had an overwhelming sense of clarity and anger. I started screaming at God, at the sky, at everyone and no one, full of fury for what had happened to me, for the situation in which I found myself. I yelled, full-lung, at the sky and the ocean. I yelled until I'd let it all out, and I couldn't yell any more.

I burst into tears. I was muddy, wet, dishevelled and broken. My clothes were torn and dirty. I must have looked like a complete maniac. I certainly felt like one. As my shouts echoed across the ocean into nothingness, a sense of calm finally washed over me. It felt like God had heard me. I quickly became preoccupied with a new mission. I had to get back to the one place that seemed normal. I had to get back to Barney's Beanery. It was not an easy mission. I was many, many miles from West Hollywood. With no phone and no money, my only way back was on foot.

I continued to stalk my way along the beach, keeping my head down. I passed stretches of expensive Malibu mansions that glowed invitingly in the night, but down at the water's edge nobody could see me. The beaches were steep and the waves broke noisily. There was no path. Mostly I found myself wading through the water, my shoes and trousers soaking wet, barely keeping my three remaining cigarettes dry. Sometimes the beach ran out and I found myself clambering over rocks to find the next section of sand. I was exhausted, both physically and mentally. I was dehydrated. I had no real idea where I was or where I was going. West Hollywood and Barney's Beanery seemed what they were: impossibly distant.

I reached a quiet and remote stretch of coastline. Slightly inland there was a gas station. I made my way towards it. I must have looked incredibly frail emerging from the ocean and approaching the only building in sight. A shadow of anything I'd been before. All I wanted was a lighter. Perhaps I might find someone here who had one.

• • •

Three people saved me that night. I think of them as my three kings. Their kindness not only helped me get back to where I needed to be, it also prompted me to come to terms with my life and what was important in it. I had no idea, as I staggered up to that unprepossessing gas station, that I was about to meet the first.

There was nobody inside apart from an elderly Indian man working the night shift behind the counter. When I asked him for a light, he was quietly apologetic. 'I'm sorry sir,' he said. 'I do not smoke.'

I stared numbly at him. Then I mumbled a couple of words of thanks and stumbled out of the gas station. I was ready to continue along the road, but then I saw that the man had followed me out. 'Are you okay?' he said.

I barely knew what to say. How could I even begin to tell him how not okay I was. Instead I just asked, croaky voiced: 'I don't suppose you have any water?'

The man pointed back into the gas station. 'Go to the chiller,' he said. 'Take one. Take a big one.'

I thanked him again and staggered into the gas station where I helped myself to a two-litre bottle of water. When I turned once more, the man was back behind his counter. 'Where are you going?' he said.

I told him. 'West Hollywood.'

'A long way.'

'Yeah.'

'You don't have any money?'

I shook my head.

The man smiled. He took out his wallet, opened it up and pulled out what I could see was his last twenty dollar bill. 'Take it,' he said.

I stared again, at him and at the twenty.

'I'm not a wealthy man,' he said quietly. 'I don't have much money. I don't have a big house. I don't have a fancy car. But I have my wife, and I have my children, and I have my grandchildren, and that means I am a *rich* man. A *very* rich man.' He fixed me with a piercing stare and inclined his head a little. 'Are *you* a rich man?' he asked.

My reflex reaction was to burst into rueful laughter. 'Rich?' I said. 'I'm a millionaire! And here I am, asking you for a bottle of water and taking your last twenty dollars.' And what I thought to myself, but did not say out loud, was: *I'm not rich at all. Not like you.*

He smiled again. 'That should get you some of the way back to West Hollywood,' he said.

'I promise,' I said, 'I'll come back and find you and repay the money.'

He shook his head. 'Don't bother,' he said. 'Pass it on, next time you see a person who needs your help.'

I was profuse with my thanks as I left the gas station. His kindness was a balm. A pick-me-up. I began to feel that

I might be successful in my mission. I continued along the Pacific Coast Highway in the pitch darkness. Every time a car passed, I ducked out of the way and hid in a bush. After a few more soggy-shoed miles, an old Ford Mustang sped past. I crouched and hid. Once it was a hundred metres away, I saw the orange glow of a cigarette butt fly out of the window and land on the road. I sprinted towards it, desperate to light one of my own damp cigarettes from that tiny spark. I reached it in time and smoked three cigarettes one after the other, each lit by the last as I hunkered down by the side of the road. I nodded to the sky and thanked God for his divine intervention. Then I carried on walking.

I met my second king at the next gas station, several more miles down the road. I was exhausted, still damp and sweaty, still bloodied and covered in dirt. I staggered into the gas station and asked the guy there if he knew anybody who could help me in my situation. The guy said no, folded his arms and asked me to leave. It was nearing midnight and there was only one car in sight, parked up - the first vehicle I'd seen for a good while. I staggered up to it and, ever so softly, tapped on the window. The driver, a young Black guy twice my size, opened the window. I started to say: 'Mate, I know this sounds weird but ...'

He shook his head. 'I'm Uber only,' he said. 'You want a ride, book me on your phone.'

But I had no phone. I had nothing but the damp, torn clothes on my back and the twenty-dollar bill the Indian man had given me. I made up a crazy story: that my girlfriend and I'd had a massive argument and she'd dropped me out here in the middle of nowhere. All I had was twenty bucks, and could he *please* see his way to taking me just as far towards West Hollywood as my money would last? I must have made a pitiful sight, and by rights he should have taken one look at me, shaken his head and rolled up his window. But he didn't. He looked me up and down, then he indicated that I should hop in the back. A seat never felt so good. 'Where do you need me to take you?' he asked.

I told him Barney's Beanery, and reiterated that I only had twenty bucks and was happy for him to drop me off when my money had run out. But he waved away my protestations. Maybe he saw that I was in no fit state to hike back to West Hollywood. Maybe, like the Indian man at the previous gas station, he was just kind. 'I'll take you there,' he said. I struggled to understand his generosity. Didn't he want a book signed? Didn't he want a picture for his kids? Nope. He just wanted to help someone in need. He took me all the way. A sixty-dollar cab ride, maybe more. I begged him to write down his name and number so that I could repay him, but again he waved me away. 'Don't worry about it, man. It's cool.'

It was half past one in the morning when he dropped me outside Barney's. I had a final, failed attempt to ask him for his number so I could pay him the proper fare, but he wouldn't hear of it. He drove down the road and out of sight. I never saw him again.

I turned towards Barney's. It was kicking-out time. Most of the clientele had left. I couldn't quite believe that, thanks to the unexpected kindness of strangers, I'd made it here. Drained and dirty, I staggered up to the front door. And there I met Nick, the bouncer. He knew me well. This was my regular hangout, after all. He looked me up and down, clearly aware that all was not as it should be. But he made no comment. He just stepped aside and said, 'You're late, dude, but if you want to come in for a quick one ...'

I entered. There were still a few regulars propping up the bar. My eyes were instantly drawn to their drinks and it struck me that I hadn't touched or even thought about alcohol for the best part of forty-eight hours. I stared vacantly, wondering why I was there. The bartender automatically put a beer on the counter. I instinctively went to grab it before realising I had no interest in that whatsoever. I backed away from the beer, back through the bar doors. Nick was kicking out the last of the drinkers. As I stared into nothingness, he asked me: 'You alright, dude?'

'Can you lend me twenty bucks?' I said. 'Just so I can get home?'

Nick gave me a long, steady stare. 'Where are your keys?' he said.

'I don't have them, mate,' I said. 'I don't have anything.' And as I said it, I remembered the voice of the Indian man at the gas station. *Are you a rich man?*

'You're coming home with me,' Nick said. 'Let's go.' I didn't question him.

Nick became my third king that night, as he took me back to his home. It was a small apartment, but it was warm and comfortable and very welcoming. He sat me down, made me endless cups of tea and then, for the next three hours, he listened to me talk. Words flooded out of me. Anxieties I had never properly articulated rose from somewhere inside me. The truth of my situation started to emerge. I confronted the one fact that I'd been too scared to admit to myself for too long: I was no longer in love with Jade. She had been instrumental in keeping my career on the road, no question. But I'd become too reliant on her, for my wellbeing and even for my opinions. It had blinded me to the uncomfortable truth that my feelings for her had changed. We wanted different things out of life. I was not being honest with her, but more importantly I was not being honest with myself. If I wanted to rescue myself, and if I wanted to do the right thing by Jade, I had to tell her the truth.

By now the sun had risen. The police, I later discovered, were out looking for me for most of the night. So were Jade and all my friends. For all they knew, I was dead somewhere in the forests of Malibu, or languishing in some prison cell. As dawn arrived, I asked to use Nick's phone. I called Jade and told her where I was.

Jade was incredibly relieved to hear my voice and find out I was okay. She came to pick me up. We went home. I sat down with her and explained how I was feeling. It was emotional and raw. I was changing the course of our lives with a single conversation. My words were not something a person says, or hears, lightly. I told her there was nothing I wouldn't do for her, for the rest of her life, and I meant it. But I'd lost my way and I needed to find it again. She accepted my explanation with a grace I probably didn't deserve. And with that, our relationship was over.

I'd spent the night searching for my way back home, and I'd come to the realisation that I wasn't there yet. The intervention had been upsetting. It had angered and confused me. But I was beginning to understand that it came from the right place and I needed to seek some help. I was going to do it for myself.

27

TIME WELL SPENT

or

VERSIONS OF MYSELF

Rehab. The word has a stigma. I don't think it should have. The few weeks I spent re-connecting with myself were some of the best and most important of my life, although I definitely didn't appreciate that at the time. My intervention had been painful and humiliating. The first facility at which I'd ended up had been the wrong place for me. But with hindsight, I'm glad I went through all that, because it led to certain epiphanies that would change my life for the better. I didn't believe that my substance use warranted the intervention, but I'm glad it happened because it briefly took me away from the world that was making me unhappy, and allowed me to get some clarity. I grew to realise that everyone in the room on the day of my intervention was there because they cared about me. Not my career, not my value. They cared about me.

After that difficult conversation with Jade I decided to check myself into a facility in the heart of the Californian countryside, miles from anywhere. It was smaller than the previous place, a family-run centre that treated a maximum of fifteen patients at a time. Far less of a medical facility, more of a sanctuary for struggling young people. There were two houses: one for boys, one for girls. The patients mostly had issues with prescription medications, and alcohol on the side. These were not the more seriously ill people I'd been forced alongside after the intervention. That's not to say that they didn't have problems: they did, and it was immediately obvious that their problems were more serious than mine. However, I immediately felt a connection with them. I didn't feel quite so out of place there.

All of a sudden there was a rigorous structure to my day. I realised that I'd missed that. Throughout my childhood, on the Harry Potter set, I'd had structure imposed upon me without me really knowing it. I was told when to turn up, where to stand, where to look, what to say. There is something calming about that kind of certainty, and when it's part of your life for such a long time, its absence can disorientate you. Now it was back. We woke at sunrise for morning gratitude, during which we would sit round in a circle and one of us would read a poem, proverb or prayer to set our intentions for the day. These would be small, achievable goals: I might have pledged, for example, to talk back less (my former cheekiness had not entirely deserted me). We would have breakfast, after which there would be hour-long classes throughout the day, with five-minute breaths of fresh air in between. Some would be group sessions, some would be solo. There would be cognitive behavioural therapy, hypnotherapy, one-on-one counselling. Sometimes we would laugh, or cry, and we would all talk openly and honestly to each other about our thoughts, our problems and what had brought us there in the first place.

The highlight of the treatment was when we were allowed to leave the facility and volunteer at a food truck for the homeless in Venice Beach. I really enjoyed the shared camaraderie of the volunteers. Some were from treatment, some were locals, some were old, some were young, but all were united in wanting to help those in need. It didn't matter who you were or what you'd done, as long as you were there to help. I loved it. (I even learned how to make a burrito, a word I'd previously only heard watching *Beavis and Butt-Head* with Ash.)

We were all complete strangers in treatment, and vulnerable in different ways. In an environment like that you quickly become very close to each other. You bond into a family. In a matter of days, you start to care deeply about your fellow patients. That in itself is a transformative experience. Before, I'd have days at home where you wouldn't be able to get me out of bed for lack of passion in anything at all. And I couldn't show compassion to anybody else because I was so consumed with my own situation. Here, painting my guitar with a stranger, or teaching them a few chords on my ukulele, became the most important things in my day-to-day life. We'd all been so open that we ended up caring more about each other than about our own problems: the ultimate mental health tool. Suddenly you are able to put clearly into perspective everything that was overwhelming you.

• • •

The rules in rehab were good for me. They helped me get myself back on track. They were also my downfall. Because, let's face it, rules had never quite been my thing.

Personal space was important. Touching was not allowed. Signs of affection were absolutely forbidden. Hugging? Forget it. It seemed odd to me at the time, although I now understand why. However, I'd just come out of a long-term relationship and there were pretty girls around me, one in particular. On a couple of occasions, the therapists caught me canoodling with her round the side of the building when we were pretending to put the bins out. One evening I committed the cardinal sin of sneaking into the girls' house, and into her room. I honestly didn't have anything particularly nefarious in mind. She had been quiet at dinner and I wanted to make sure she was okay. When I heard a knock on the door, though, I was terrified at the prospect of being rumbled and reprimanded. I hit the deck and rolled under the bed to hide. The door opened. I held my breath. I saw a pair of shoes stepping in my direction. They stopped at the edge of the bed. A moment of awkward silence, and then a woman's upside-down face appeared. I gave what I hoped was a winning smile and, with a mini-wave, squeaked: 'Hi!'

'What's going on?'

'Nothing!'

'Why are you underneath her bed?'

'No reason!'

I have to admit it didn't look good. The woman looked at me with disappointed eyes, not dissimilar to my mum's when I was arrested that time.

I was allowed out the next day to record a voiceover for an animation. I'd been in treatment at the facility for three weeks. I was completely sober, mind sharp as ever, cogs well oiled, full of positivity. The interventionist picked me up and took me to the studio. When I finished, I was on cloud nine. But before I got into the car he told me that I wasn't allowed to continue my treatment. I would have to go back to the facility, where my stuff had already been packed, and leave without saying goodbye to anyone. I had not impressed them with my schoolboy antics.

I was upset, and angry too. I burst into tears and kicked a fence. When we returned to the facility, I begged them not to kick me out. I spent hours reeling off all the reasons why they should let me stay. I collapsed onto the floor in tears. I tried to persuade them that they were making a mistake and I would do better. But they were unyielding. I'd broken the rules too many times, they said. I was disrupting the others' recoveries. I had to go.

I spent the following week in a daze. I'd spent time in a whole new world, with a group of people I cared deeply about. Suddenly I couldn't be part of that group, and I missed them. But those three weeks had been life-changing. I realised that before I had been existing in a state of absolute numbness. It wasn't that I was ready to jump off a bridge; it was that jumping off a bridge and winning the lottery seemed like equivalent outcomes. I had no interest in anything, good or bad. You could have told me that I was going to be the next James Bond, and I wouldn't have cared. Now, I had my emotions back and they were firing on all cylinders. Some emotions were good. Some were bad. But either were better than none at all.

• • •

They could ask me to leave the treatment centre. They could bar me from saying goodbye to my family there. But they couldn't stop me volunteering every Thursday at the food truck in Venice Beach.

I didn't really know where else to go or what else to do. The boardwalk at Venice Beach can be an intimidating place full of intimidating people, homeless and struggling. When you offer them free food from a truck, you're met with timid, suspicious responses. But they are so very grateful for it afterwards, and I found it incredibly rewarding to be part of that. But I was directionless myself, so when I saw an old friend of mine while I was volunteering on the boardwalk, and he asked me to dinner at his place that night, I gratefully accepted.

His name was Greg Cipes: an actor, voiceover artist and modern-day activist for animals and the planet. He lived in a tiny apartment on the boardwalk with his dog Wingman. He's a vegan. He doesn't drink and doesn't smoke. He's the cleanest, most accepting man I've ever met. I thought, *This could be a good place to stay for a couple of nights.* A couple of nights turned into a couple of months, sleeping on a yoga mat on his floor, with the sometimes disconcerting sounds of the boardwalk at night outside, and Wingman waking me at six every morning by licking my face. That time truly reprogrammed who I was as a person.

Greg referred to his swims in the ocean as a re-set. He taught me that every decision was always better made after the re-set. I resisted it at first, but after a couple of weeks I embraced his philosophy. We re-set at least twice a day, morning and evening. Before running into the ocean, we'd put our hands to the sky, say a short prayer and take three very deep breaths, before proceeding to run in, whooping like the children we are at heart. Greg also taught me that when you're coming out of the water you should raise your hands to the sky and say thank you, to show gratitude for everything you have in your life. Greg told me that Einstein had appeared to him in a dream, saying that walking backwards off the beach would create new neural pathways. So we always walked backwards off the beach, keeping our eyes on the ocean, picking up pieces of littered plastic along the way. 'Try to leave every environment better than when you found it,' he told me.

Greg also liked to talk to the seagulls. At first I thought this was ridiculous. In a very friendly, high-pitched voice, he'd tell them: 'You're so beautiful! You're doing a great job!' I didn't join him at first and to be honest I thought he was slightly mad. He then went on to tell me his theory that seagulls are the smartest birds in the world. When I asked him why, he said, 'Name another bird that spends so much time at the beach!' I couldn't argue with that, and now I do all the above as a daily routine whenever I'm in LA.

Some people think Greg is a little crazy. He has long hippie hair, eccentric homemade clothing, is always carrying Wingman - who he refers to as his guru - and speaks slowly and incredibly calmly in sometimes cryptic sentences. But no one has shown me more unconditional kindness, generosity and understanding. No one has taught me more about myself and endlessly shows me new ways to find the light.

Greg would argue he taught me nothing. He was just a witness.

• • •

After a few months with Greg I decided, at the age of thirty-one, to get my own Venice Beach shack and start my life again. I got new clothes - mostly from thrift stores, mostly floral. I rescued a Labrador called Willow. I was able to enjoy being myself again. Not Tom the celebrity with the house in the hills. Not Tom with the orange Lamborghini. The other Tom. The Tom who had good things to offer. I went to the beach every day. I took acting jobs that I wanted to do rather than being pressured by other people's opinions of what I should be doing. Most importantly, I regained control of my decision-making. I didn't go out for the sake of going out, or because other people were telling me to. Life was better than ever.

So when one day, a couple of years later, the numbness returned, without any warning and with no particular trigger, it was a shock. There was no rhyme or reason to it. I just suddenly and unexpectedly found it almost impossible to find reasons to get out of bed. If I hadn't had Willow to look after I probably wouldn't have emerged from under the covers very much at all. I endured that feeling for a while, telling myself this will pass, before accepting that it simply wasn't going to. I decided that I had to do something proactive to stop myself feeling - or *not* feeling - like this anymore.

I fought the notion of rehab first time round. But this wasn't the same me. I'd grown to accept my genetic predisposition to these changes of mood, rather than refusing to acknowledge them. I relinquished all command and, with a little help from my friends, I found somewhere I could seek help. I can honestly say it was one of the hardest decisions I ever had to make. But the very fact that I was able to admit to myself that

I needed some help - and I was going to do something about it - was an important moment.

I am not alone in having these feelings. Just as we all experience physical ill-health at some stage in our lives, so we all experience mental ill-health too. There's no shame in that. It's not a sign of weakness. And part of the reason that I took the decision to write these pages is the hope that by sharing my experiences, I might be able to help someone else who is struggling. I learned in the first facility that helping others is a powerful weapon in the fight against mood disorders. Another effective tool is talking about all your thoughts and emotions, not just the fluffy ones. I found that easier to do in an American culture. We Brits are more reserved, and sometimes see talking about our feelings as indulgent. In fact, it's essential. So here goes. I'm no longer shy of putting my hands up and saying: I'm not okay. To this day I never know which version of myself I'm going to wake up to. It can happen that the smallest chores or decisions - brushing my teeth, hanging up a towel, should I have tea or coffee - overwhelm me. Sometimes I find the best way to get through the day is by setting myself tiny, achievable goals that take me from one minute to the next. If you sometimes feel like that, you are not alone, and I urge you to talk about it to someone. It's easy to bask in the sun, not so easy to enjoy the rain. But one can't exist without the other. The weather always changes. Feelings of sadness and happiness deserve equal mental screen time.

Which takes us back to the concept of rehab, and the stigma attached to the word. By no means do I want to casualise the idea of therapy - it's a difficult first step to take - but I do want to do my bit to normalise it. I think we all need it in one shape or another, so why wouldn't it be normal to talk openly about how we're feeling? 'I'm happy we won the footy.' 'I'm pissed off the ref didn't give that penalty.' 'I'm so excited to see who they sign next.' If we apply such a passionate tongue and eager ear to something like football, for instance, why wouldn't we do the same about the unspoken stuff? 'I couldn't get out of bed this morning because everything felt too much.' 'I don't know what I'm doing with my life.' 'I know I'm loved, so why do I feel so lonely?' Rather than see therapy as the emergency consequence of excess or illness, we should start to see it for what it can be: an essential opportunity to take time out from the voices in your head, the pressures of the world and the expectations we place on ourselves. It doesn't have to be thirty days in a rehabilitation centre. It can be thirty hours over an entire year talking to someone about your feelings, or thirty minutes to set positive intentions for the day, or thirty seconds to breathe and remind yourself that you are here and you are now. If rehab is nothing more than time devoted to looking after yourself, how can that not be time well spent?

Afterword

Which brings us back to the present, and to London where I live now. As I write these pages, my adventures in LA are behind me and in some ways it feels as though I've come full circle. My life is more settled now. More ordinary. I wake each morning, full of gratitude, in my house among the leafy heaths of North London. I put in my earphones to listen to the morning's news while I walk Willow, who is seemingly on constant squirrel patrol. Back home I'll make myself a ham and cheese sandwich (I still have the palate of a nine-year-old) and I'll spend some time reading scripts or playing music. Then I'll get on my bike to cycle into the West End, where I find myself performing on stage for the first time.

The play is *2:22 A Ghost Story*, and before each performance, as I prepare to step out on to the stage, I can't help but reflect on the importance stories have had in my life, and on the value they hold for so many people. It would be easy to dismiss them. I nearly did just that when, two decades ago, I lined up with a bunch of young hopefuls all wanting to be cast in the story of a boy who lived in a cupboard under the stairs. It didn't seem like much of a story to me. Frankly, I thought it was a bit ridiculous-sounding. Now, of course, I see things differently. We live in a world where we seem increasingly in need of ways to unify ourselves, ways to build bridges and feel as one. It strikes me that very few things have achieved those aims as successfully as the brilliant world of Harry Potter. Not a day goes by that I don't receive a message from fans all over the world telling me just that.

To be part of those stories is humbling, and feels like an extraordinary honour. It makes me more ambitious than ever to harness the power of art and storytelling so that I can pass on the baton to another generation.

It surprises some people that I've never re-read the Harry Potter books, or even watched the films in their entirety apart from at the premieres. From time to time I've been in front of the TV with some friends and one of the movies has come on, prompting the obligatory piss-taking of 'Harry Potter Wanker' and 'Broomstick Prick'. But I've never sat down on purpose to watch them, beginning to end. It's nothing to do with a lack of pride. Quite the opposite. It's because I'm saving them for the moment that I look forward to most in my future: one day sharing these stories - books first, then the films - with my own little Muggles.

Several years ago, on that night when I busted out of rehab and trekked alone and confused along the Malibu coastline, the first of my three kings asked me a question: 'Are you a rich man?' I barely knew how to answer. I'm not sure I entirely understood the question. He told me he was a rich man, not because he had wealth but because he had his family around him. He knew what was important in life. He knew no amount of money, fame or praise would ever make him content. He knew to help people, and it would naturally pass on to others.

Now I understand that too. The only true currency we have in life is the effect we have on those around us.

I know my life has been a fortunate one. I will always be grateful to and proud of the films that gave me so many opportunities. I'm even prouder of the fans who keep the wizarding world's flame burning brighter than ever. And I try to remind myself every day how lucky I am to have my life. A life where love, family and friendship are at the forefront. It's not lost on me that the importance of these is one of the great lessons of the Harry Potter stories. The realisation of this is what makes me a very rich man indeed.

Acknowledgements

Thanks to the witches and wizards at Ebury, especially Claire Collins, Andrew Goodfellow, Charlotte Hardman, Jessica Anderson, Patsy O'Neill, Shelise Robertson, Sarah Scarlett, Rebecca Jones and Jeanette Slinger, for all their hard work making this happen. To my literary agent Stephanie Thwaites and all at Curtis Brown. To my French and quadratic equations teacher Adam Parfitt, for your patience and skill with the quill.

To all the fan groups across the world, especially the girls at feltbeats.com, for their tireless support. To John Alcantar, for introducing me to Comic Cons and holding my hand around the world. To my team - Gary O'Sullivan, Cliff Murray, Justin Grey Stone, Allison Band, Steven Gersh, Jamie Feldman, Scott Womack and Romilly Bowlby - for always looking out for me. To the people who helped along the way: Anne Bury, Sue Abacus, Maxine Hoffman, Michael Duff, Nina Gold, Peter Hewitt, Andy Tennant, Chris Columbus, Alfonso Cuarón, Mike Newell, David Yates, Kevin Reynolds, Amma Asante, Charlie Stratton, Sara Sugarman and Rachel Talalay. To Joseph Fiennes, Andy Serkis, Paul Hodge, Sam Swainsbury, Grant Gustin and the late Dave Legeno, for all taking me under their wing at one point or another. To Jason Isaacs, for being the best second-round dad a son could ask for. To Richie Jackson, Melissa Tamschick and her mum Anne, Tessa Davies, Michael Eagle-Hodgson, Stevie, Rob and Nina Challens, Matt 'Chef'

Whites, Dan Raw and all the crew, for the great memories I have growing up. To Jade, Stevie G and all the Gordon family, for taking me in with open arms.

To Derek Pitts, for being my b ... b ... brother. To Greg Cipes, for teaching me how to talk to the seagulls. To Daniel Radcliffe and Rupert Grint, for all the years at Hogwarts and beyond. To Emma Watson, for quacking with me all these years. To everyone who worked on the Potter films, for helping to shape who I am today. To my brothers, for keeping this maggot's feet on the ground. To my grandparents, especially Gramps and Wendy Bird, for all the encouragement in discovering the wonders of life. To my beloved Seahorse, for being my lighthouse every day and teaching me bassoon.

Finally, to my mum and dad, for absolutely everything.